Church Greeters 101

Putting the Pieces Together for an Effective

Greeting Team and Ministry

Rev. Christopher Walker

I've read through the book and my mind is swirling with ideas. There is so much to talk about to our greeters and ushers at our meeting on later this month!!!!

Church Greeters 101
Putting the Pieces Together for an Effective Greeting Team and Ministry

Author: Chris Walker
Copyright © 2013, 3rd Edition, Chris Walker

EvangelismCoach.org
9962 Brook Road #648
Glen Allen VA 23059
Visit our website at http://www.EvangelismCoach.org

Print Edition
ISBN 13: 978-0615802565 (EvangelismCoach Press)
ISBN 10: 0615802567
Printed in the United States of America

Book Design by Quick Graphics, Anchorage Alaska
Editing by Steve Strickler

Third Edition: (June 2013)
10 9 8 7 6 5 4 3

All tweets are real and quoted in this material are considered public domain. I have screenshots of every one. I have removed user names. Names of people involved in my stories have all been removed for privacy.

Scripture citations come from The Holy Bible : New International Version. 1996, (online electronic edition). Grand Rapids: Zondervan. Used by permission.

Some of this content can be found on www.EvangelismCoach.org and related websites, but to save you time and effort they have been compiled and reformatted into one bundled e-book for you. All content original to Chris Walker.

The information in this book is only for educational purposes and is not intended as legal advice or anything other than information.

For the past 8 years, I've lead the Welcome Ministry Teams in my church. How to be a church greeter seems like common sense to me, but to many people it's not. Your book was most helpful in giving me training ideas.

Kevin Cunningham
EncourageAndEquip.com
Nashua NH

I've been looking for a resource to help guide me as I work to rebuild our greeter ministry. Church Greeters 101 hits the spot! What I really found helpful about Church Greeters 101 was the practical action steps in each chapter. By the time I finished, I could see how to put together an effective greeter training, which was what I was needing. After reading this book, I could tell that Chris has been listening to the people he seeks to serve. The practical nature of this book has given me the boost I needed to rebuild our greeter ministry.

'Bobby G' Griffiths
Worship, Arts & Media Coach

Many thanks. Book was just the thing I had been looking for as I am trying to improve the Meeting & Greeting at our Anglican Church. The book is certainly comprehensive and is very suitable for our two congregations of 50 – 80 each. It will help to change the process from being a 'chore' to 'enjoyable'.

Roger Street
Whangaparaoa, New Zealand.

There are a lot of articles and books on 'why' greeters are so important to the vitality of a church, but Pastor Walker gives us insight and guidance on the 'how' of organizing a vital greeter ministry. A great primer for churches organizing church greeter training — filled with practical workshop guidelines and training exercises.

Roger Bridgeman
First Congregational Church Outreach Committee
Sharon, Massachusetts.

Table of Contents

Introduction

Tonight I was asked by a guy in our church to be a "Greeter" which means I'd shake people's hands as they come in. (Twitter user)

A greeter does more than shake hands on a Sunday morning.

Greeters are the front line of your church's hospitality ministry. They are a vital part of your organized friendliness that helps members and visitors connect with each other.

Too many churches simply recruit warm bodies to fill this role. When those jobs are filled without much thought, training, or planning, it indicates the failure to recognize the special role that greeters have in welcoming your guests and members.

Why another book on church greeters?

After six years of writing on church hospitality issues for EvangelismCoach.org, reading several different books on greeting ministry, conducting live workshops on church hospitality, and interacting with users of ChurchGreeterTraining.com, I've noticed the following holes in the information:

- How to organize a greeting ministry

- How to train your greeters / ushers

- And the big one: Greeters want to know what to say.

After all, there are only so many ways one can say "Good morning" at the entry door greeting line.

As part of my work, I've talked with several church leaders around the United States who are at the point of organizing some kind of greeting team. They have ushers at the sanctuary doors, but no greeters at the entry doors. These churches consider themselves to be friendly, but they want to take that friendliness to the next level.

Other churches simply ignore this blessing of hospitality because they either fail to see the need to greet visitors, lack the know-how for how to greet visitors, or simply don't care and prefer to maintain things the way they are.

Specialization in Training

According to anecdotal surveys that I've done with leaders of greeting ministries, it is clear that currently available material for greeter training is not specialized enough. The information on the market now is not answering the questions asked of me.

With the exception of two books on the market as of late 2009, much of what I have read contains outdated practices that are not even relevant for today.

Some books I've evaluated are focused on large campus churches in the American suburbs. However, nearly 80% of churches in the US see fewer than 100 in worship attendance on a regular basis. One recent statistic pushes this further, claiming the average worship attendance in

America is only 53 people. These books miss the general church audience.

Some resources are focused on the overall picture of hospitality and first impressions that greeters might only get one or two pages of mention. These books don't fill the gap in recruiting or training.

This book, in contrast, seeks to fill in that gap and give you some practical steps in training your greeters. This book's target audience is greeters, hospitality committees, and those who want to ramp up their greeting process to the next level. We don't have to be perfect, but continue to grow towards a higher level of excellence. Ongoing training provides growth in that direction.

We greet the guests who come to our homes. We help them feel welcome and we tend to their needs. In a similar fashion, all of your church's hospitality ministers help members and visitors to your church feel welcome and have their needs met. It is what Les Parrott calls "Organized Friendliness" (Serving as a Church Greeter, 13).

You want your greeters to assist in the overall first impressions of your church. You want your greeters to increase the quality of the welcome experience. And, you want **your greeters to have fun in the process** of serving the church and serving the people who enter your doors.

Choice of terms

The available literature seems to be split over the use of the term "greeter." Some books use it without argument or any further thought. Other books prefer the word "host" to reflect more of the language of hospitality, since the role of greeters goes beyond saying hello. If language choice is important to you and your context, pick the word you will use. For this book, I'll simply work with greeter because it is more common.

What this book is not

In this book, I intentionally focus on recruiting and training church greeters and ushers: the volunteer side of your church's hospitality ministry. This book is intended as a manual and reference for greeter coordinators, hospitality committees, and greeter volunteers. I've provided appendices to print out and use for training material.

This particular text does not go into marketing to get visitors, general first impressions ministry, and assimilation strategies. My other eBook (PDF Download only), which is found at http://www.WelcomeChurchVisitors.com, focuses more on the big picture of hospitality ministries–creating a good first impression (presentation of the building, the visitor experience and wow factor). It has one small chapter on greeters. This book you are reading now elaborates more in depth about these important volunteers.

This information has developed and refined after years of reading, research and conversation with many church pastors and hospitality committees around the United States and some in Latin America. I want to give them a giant word of thanks for talking with me on the telephone and by email, allowing me to pick their brains, and to learn what works and doesn't.

This material also reflects the cross cultural work I do in Latin America and Spanish language churches. As I experience church in two very different cultures, I see differences that often provide insights into why we do things that we do.

Action Steps

After many of these chapters, you'll see a section called action steps. These are meant to spur some kind of next action as you seek to grow and develop your ministry. Feel free to use them in your next meeting with your hospitality committee. You can modify them to suit your own context.

I want to give you two items you can do right now. First, this book and teaching will be updated. The best way to stay up to date is to like the EvangelismCoach Facebook Page. I'll let you know about any updates there. I'll also be sharing some daily encouragement and thoughts about hospitality, evangelism, and discipleship. To like the EvangelismCoach.org Facebook page, visit http://www.Facebook.com/EvangelismCoach

Secondly, you can also visit http://www.ChurchGreeterTraining.com and signup to ten free videos I've created by email that focus on greeter tips you can send to your greeters. Look for the free video tab. You'll need to enter your name and email to register and once you've done that, you'll be able to watch the first video right away, called "The Six Most Dangerous Words."

Please be sure that your email is completely safe with me. It allows me to send the free videos in a sequence. It will not be shared with anyone else. At the bottom of every email I will send, there will be an unsubscribe link where you can drop out of future videos and announcements of greeter training materials that I continue to create.

So before going any further, make sure you visit http://www.ChurchGreeterTraining.com to start getting those videos.

Chapter 1.

Church Greeting as Specialized Ministry

Over the last few decades in the United States, the role of the church greeter has taken on a larger importance and has become a vital ministry expression of the local church. How did it get there? Greeter ministry is one of those innovations that has stuck around and is now a cultural expectation in North America. It has been a ministry in the church for so long that its absence would be noteworthy. As I see it, the ministry of greeting is now an operating assumption, and it seems to have its roots in the North American church growth movement, the development of the consumer experience, and some biblical precedence.

This doesn't mean that all churches have started a greeting ministry. Perhaps the operating assumption is that all members are to give a welcome. Or perhaps your church is small enough that a warm greeting naturally occurs without any need for organizing a team. But as growth happens, some organization of greeters will likely happen.

Some might be new church developments that are so visitor focused that greeting happens naturally. Yet even these churches will eventually need some systems organization to keep up the first impressions ministry and greet both members and visitors who walk in the front door.

My experience

Let me tell you a little of my experience. I think back to the rare times I went to church as a child in the 1970s and early 1980s. My family remembers that the pastor (sometimes with his wife) would stand at the exit doors to greet our family as we left the sanctuary. People would complement him with "Nice job, pastor" or "You really preached a good one today." Exiting the sanctuary wasn't the place to trade a whole lot of words as a few hundred people were trying to leave in a pretty quick pace.

I became a Christian in mid 1980s during my teenage years. I started attending church on my own. Once I got my driver's license, I regularly attended church. I remember two or three people standing at the front door, extending their hand to mine, shaking hands with me, and sometimes asking me how was I doing. I remember and treasure some of the friendships that I formed with adults. One of those adult greeters turned into a mentor who shaped the direction of my ministry. He died of cancer 3 years after I met him, but his influence reached far beyond shaping the life of a kid.

As that church grew to be one of the largest Methodist congregations in the area, the church started recruiting families to serve as front door greeters. As the campus grew to have multiple entry points, they recruited church members to serve at the various doorways during multiple Sunday morning services. To manage all of their recruiting, they developed the specialized role of a greeter recruiter, filled by a volunteer.

I remember being called by a volunteer coordinator and asked if I'd like to serve as a greeter. I felt privileged to welcome people to our church and enjoyed greeting people as they walked in from the parking lot. The pace of people entering was slow enough at times that I could make some small talk with people as they walked in. Some were friends that I looked forward to seeing every week while others were strangers that I wanted to welcome. This was easy for me and suited my personality well. I didn't need a whole lot of training because it was easy for me to greet people and say hello. (Some of your greeters may be more nervous than I was).

In spite of the Methodist influence in my formative years of my Christian faith, I became an ordained pastor in the Presbyterian tribe in 1997. The two churches I served recruited greeters without ever asking why. It was something the church did. The ministry of greeters was an operating assumption.

In my current ministry, I get to preach in other churches. I typically meet greeters when I enter the facility. Because of my interest in this subject, I notice when a door greeter is absent, or the hospitality center is not staffed, or when a greeter doesn't bother to make eye contact. I observe what seems to work and not work. I have preached in many churches that still have the practice of the pastor standing at the exit door to shake the hands of people as they exit.

In my role as a church growth and evangelism trainer who teaches all over the US and Latin America, I get to experience different styles of greeting and innovations in greeting ministry, in two different cultures. It is rare when I'm not greeted at the door, at the visitor center and unless it's a mega church, it is rare when I'm not greeted by the pastor while leaving the sanctuary or church. If I preached that morning, I'm invited to stand with the pastor at the exit door to greet the departing parishioners and visitors.

Even in the Latin American churches I visit, a majority of them organize volunteers who fulfill the functions of a greeter, even if there is no equivalent word in Spanish. These people open the door for you, hand you the Sunday bulletin, and say such ritualized greetings like "Dios le bendiga" (God bless you) and "Bienvenido" (Welcome). Many will wear uniforms as they proudly fulfill their role, even if the tropical humidity is oppressive.

In July of 2009, I preached in Central Presbyterian Church in Guatemala City, Guatemala. When I entered the sanctuary, women in blue uniforms wearing name tags and the Presbyterian seal as a lapel pin extended a hand and greeted me and our team as we entered. At the end of the service, I was escorted to the principal door where people filed out. As I stood there with the pastor, I shook the hands of what felt like one thousand people that day.

A Ministry with Biblical Roots

In the Scriptures, we see the term 'doorkeeper.' The doorkeeper is the one who would open the door to permit people to enter, or keep the door closed to keep people out.

We find in the Psalms where one writer talks about being a doorkeeper in the house of the Lord. Psalm 84:10 says

> *Better is one day in your courts than a thousand elsewhere; I would rather be a doorkeeper in the house of my God than dwell in the tents of the wicked.*

Levites were doorkeepers to the ark (1 Chronicles 15:23-24). We see more stories of doorkeepers in 2 Kings 7:10-11, and 11:4-9. Their duties were to guard the city gates, temple, and large buildings. They were in charge of admitting or rejecting visitors. We see the pride that a family took in the generational service as a doorkeeper:

Shallum son of Kore, the son of Ebiasaph, the son of Korah, and his fellow gatekeepers from his family (the Korahites) were responsible for guarding the thresholds of the Tent just as their fathers had been responsible for guarding the entrance to the dwelling of the Lord (1 Chronicles 9:19).

In the New Testament, the Greek word for doorkeeper is *thyroros*. Used in Mark 13:34, the word refers to the servant assigned the task to watch the door for the man who is going away. In John 10:3, the doorkeeper is the one who opens the door for the true shepherd.

A female doorkeeper let the disciple John into the house of the high priest, but kept Peter from entering. John intervened and she let Peter enter. She eventually accused Peter of knowing Jesus (John 18:15-18). Rhoda may have been a doorkeeper, being the one who answered the door when Peter escaped from Prison (Acts 12:13). In that day and time, these gatekeepers played a protective safety function, as the first line of defense in letting strangers in.

The Evolution of Specialized Ministry

Les Parrot, in his older book <u>Serving as a Church Greeter</u>, tells how greeters came to be a vital part of the ministry of local churches. Churches didn't provide greeters. Many churches did not have staff other than the pastor.

In the 1800s, most US church buildings did not have Christian education wings or family life centers. As common programs developed over the years with specialized ministries, such as youth groups, choirs, Sunday school programs, eventually the specialized ministry of ushers and greeters came into existence.

Parrott also observes that there was a shift in business philosophy after World War II away from the product itself and towards the customer experience. This shift in business culture and orientation has likely influenced the rise of practices of greeters and ushers in the church (Serving as a Church Greeter, 11-12).

Lessons from the Retail / Corporate World

The entire hospitality industry is focused on making a good first impression. Practically every industry that deals with live human customers (versus virtual customers on the Internet) cares that the customer is treated well, respected, and experiences a good interaction with the business. By creating a good experience, business owners want to make it easy for you to buy.

For example, walk into any quality hotel and the doorkeeper will greet you, likely open the door for you, and give you an enthusiastic welcome. You'll likely be greeted as well by a friendly person behind a counter. One time, I had just made it to my room when the front desk called to make sure that I had found everything in order. That was a greeting beyond what I ever expected.

On another trip, some friends and I ate dinner in a restaurant outside of Atlanta, Georgia. The *maître d'* greeted us with a smile, and asked if this was our first visit to this restaurant. Without a thought, we said yes. That triggered a chain reaction of greetings – our waitress greeted us with "We're so glad you decided to give us a try tonight, and I personally want to welcome you. I'd like to introduce you to our menu since you've not been here before." The manager came over and visited our table for a few minutes of chit chat, but not in an obtrusive way.

The greeting from the staff stood out in my mind. I recall this more than the very expensive fish! Their greeting made it likely that I'd return to that restaurant if I needed to take someone to a more upscale dinner than most neighborhood chain restaurants.

I do business in many different retail stores, hotels, coffee shops, and so on, and I'm greeted often. While it may seem casual and informal, the effect of a friendly smile and the offer of a shopping cart often put me in a better mood. Other times, I don't even notice a greeter's presence as they hand me a cart.

Greeters are part of the customer care experience in the business world and have become part of the cultural expectation in the church world. Les Parrot is right in this regard. With new business emphasis on the customer experience, this mentality has become part of the church world, and I think rightly so.

Are Church Greeters a North American concept?

At least in the US and the places I've been to in Latin America, greeters have become part of the standard practice of churches. Door greeters, hospitality center staff, ushers, parking lot greeters, Sunday school class greeters, are all part of the volunteer system that helps shape a visitor's impression of your church.

As I look at the term "greeter" I see specialized vocabulary as the ministry of greeters has matured over the last 50 years. Words are created when specialization develops or new products develop. For example, Google is now a verb. The social networking tool Twitter has a whole vocabulary. Even 'Web 2.0' has made it into the dictionary.

I sometimes see things through the lens of translation since I do evangelism training in two cultures on two continents in two languages

(English and Spanish). "How do I translate that concept or word into the other language?" "What is the word for that?"

I discovered the noun "greeter" does not appear to have a translatable equivalent in Spanish, suggesting that the evolution of the term for the specialized ministry of greeter has not yet occurred with its own vocabulary in Spanish. As I've recently worked with interpreters in nine different countries, I've encountered several attempts to translate this word:

- Saludador(a) – one who gives greetings, derivative of the verb *saludar* – to say hello.
- Recibidor(a) – one who receives; derivative of the verb *recibir* – to receive.
- Un miembro del equipo de protocól – a member of the protocol team.
- Él/La que da la bienvenida. – the one who gives a welcome.
- Portero - A literal translation of the word *doorkeeper*.
- Diácono – the word for deacon.

In contrast, the word for usher seems to have had a development that has a standard equivalent in Spanish. I've not been in enough countries or churches to know if there are other words, but the standard Spanish word I've encountered within churches in the 9 countries where I have taught is "ujier." It appears to me that this is a religious word, as the word used for ushers in theaters or opera halls is something different.

As I've talked with various pastors in various countries about "*ujieres*" I have a conversation similar to this:

Me: Who are those people at the doors who shake hands as you walk in? Do you call them ujieres?

Pastor: No, they are not ujieres.

Me: What do you call them then?

As you can see, I'm often told that those servants at the doors who welcome people are not ushers (so there is a vocabulary distinction). But when I ask what they call "greeters," I get one of the various answers listed above.

Since the word for greeter has not yet found a standard equivalent in Latin America Spanish, this may suggest that the specialized ministry of greeters is something that developed as an outgrowth of North America church growth studies under the influence of the hospitality industry. This is just an observation. Some form of greeting is found in all cultures. If you have travelled internationally, you have experienced different styles of greeting, different ways of saying hello, and different ways of expressing closeness in the form of saying hello.

Even if there isn't a specialized word in a local vocabulary for "greeter," the act of greeting in the local church remains one of the most important pieces of your church's hospitality. A friendly face and a warm hello speak volumes!

Are Greeters Necessary?

Is a greeter ministry appropriate in a church? As I've thought more about the issue, one possible angle from which to view this question is to examine the purpose of the church.

Some traditions in the body of Christ argue that the visible Church is the local expression of the invisible Church. Therefore, the church is only for believers. The pastor preaches to believers for the encouragement and edification of the church and little effort is made to invite non-believers into the mix. If a non-believer makes it in, the preaching to the believers should be so convicting that the sinner repents anyway. The church is for church people and thus greeters are not necessary.

Other traditions argue that the local church is the best place for people searching for God to find a caring community of faithful believers who can help them along in their discovery of Jesus. The pastor will mix up the preaching for both believers and seekers. A lot of effort is made at helping members invite non-believers to the church. The church is for believers and non-believers alike on their journey towards Christ. Non-believers are welcomed and encouraged to attend. Greeters are a friendly face to help people feel comfortable.

Still other traditions focus on reaching the unchurched. This leaves some believers wanting more depth of biblical teaching, greater depth in worship. The pastor teaches life lessons from the Bible, often in a short series. More pre-believers are often in attendance and even serving as volunteers while they are on their journey to Christ. I've been part of a church plant aimed at this group. Believers from other places find their way to us, but don't stay long because "we are not feeding them." The only believers that stay in churches like these tend to have an evangelistic vision of the church as life saving station for people who don't yet know Christ. Greeters help prepare the way for the message to be heard.

Church greeters serve a vital function of expressing the welcome of Christ to those who enter your church building. Part of the purpose of a church greeter is to help prepare the way for a person to encounter God in the worship service. A friendly smile might change a negative attitude. An expression of compassionate care might calm the nerves of stressed parents. A gentle welcome and genuine conversation may help people feel a sense of connection. While the simple action alone may not change the world, attentive greeters may help prepare the way for your visitor to hear more from the Lord.

Ushers as distinct from Greeters

As I look at the various books that are currently available on the open market (see Recommended Reading section at the end), there are specialized books on the work of an usher as distinct from the work of a greeter. Some books contain both. Others focus specifically on the work of an usher. The general functional distinction I make is that the ushers are primarily responsible for the activity inside the sanctuary or worship space:

- Count the offering.
- Guide people to their seats.
- Hand out bulletins or programs.
- Plan the mechanics of the offering.
- Locate the offering collection devices.
- Monitor rules of etiquette and decorum.
- Assist the pastor in ministry during the altar calls.
- Provide blankets for those who are "rested in the spirit."
- Keep people from heckling the pastor during the service.

- Remove the unruly or attend to disruptions during the service.

The greeters are primarily responsible for the sphere of activity outside the sanctuary in the foyer, entryway, atrium or lobby. Greeters are stationed by the front door, at the hospitality center and available to wander the halls as needed to provide personal escort to first time visitors. Greeters make the special effort to notice first time visitors when the service is over.

Both ushers and greeters are involved in the work of greeting people who come to your church and are covered by the scope of this book. I do have a small section on ushers for their particular work in the sanctuary (Chapter 7), but most of these principles of greeting members and visitors can apply to them as well.

Action Steps – Chapter 1

Before you get too far into implementing changes, or creating new programs, take a few moments to assess the state of your current ministry of greeting. Consider all those volunteers who are serving as greeters and ushers, as well as any volunteers serving in the administrative side of your hospitality ministry.

1. How many volunteers do you have actively serving as greeters / ushers? Get a list of names and contact information for reference.

2. If your church has a training program, what material do you use? How often is it used? If it has been a while since it was used, does anyone know where it is?

3. How often are you giving new greeter training sessions? When are your trainings held? What has been used in the past for training?

4. Is your current training program effective? What is missing that you think should be covered?

5. What is your current recruiting process and how is it accomplished? What are the mechanics of recruiting people?

6. Who has been doing the recruiting in the past? What can you learn from them about their challenges and successes? Call them and ask them.

7. This Sunday, take some time to observe the greeting process in your church. Make notes about what you observe and what you think is working right or not working at all.

8. Contact your current volunteers one by one and ask their thoughts on how they like what they are doing, what is working, and what they wish they had known before they started. Ask what isn't working for them. Ask them where they would like more training.

9. If you are a greeter volunteer, think about the last time you served. What impression of your church do you think you gave? What attitude was in your heart that day you served?

Chapter 2.

The Impact of Church Greeters

> *I look for friendliness, not just the handshake but someone asking about me. Commenter at the blog.*

One night over dinner, I heard this story firsthand from an Hispanic immigrant who had experienced the transforming grace of Christ. He had begun looking for a church for his family. He told me:

> *I had only been a Christian for six months. We moved from [another city] and began to look for a Spanish language church. I didn't find any for a few weeks, so my wife and I decided to attend an English language congregation.*
>
> *We arrived and sat down in the pews, clearly the stranger. We didn't speak English at the time, so we really had no clue as to what was happening. When the service was over, all the people began leaving.*
>
> *We stood around, and guess what? No one talked to us.*

The only thing my friend only remembers about that church six years later is that no one said hello.

Imagine your experience if you walked into a church for the first time and no one greeted you. If you were the first time visitor, imagine no one answering your questions about where the rest room is, or where you take your children. Imagine there is no one to help you with the spiritual need that drew you to church today. Imagine the feeling of sensing the congregation ignoring you.

As a regular attendee or member of a church, imagine that you have had a really awful week. Imagine there is no one at the door to notice the burden you carry and offer to pray with you. Imagine that no one cares to notice your fallen countenance that suggests you have come to church with a need. When you carry a deep emotional burden, it shows. Artaxerxes noticed Nehemiah's fallen countenance when Nehemiah entered his presence (Nehemiah 2).

Imagine for a moment that a life crisis has hit and you have not been physically or emotionally able to attend church for a few weeks. Imagine that no one has noticed your absence.

Now, how does it feel to walk into such a church? How do you characterize it? Cold? Uncaring? You would feel out of place, and you would likely feel that no one cares. If this were your first visit, you would not likely return for a second or third time.

Before any worship service begins, the work of your effective greeters helps your first time visitors and members feel welcome into the house of God.

Greeters say the craziest things.

What are your greeters known for? What impression do visitors get? Twitter provides me real life commentary of various church greeter experiences. Here are some I gathered in 2012:

- Ok, went to church & this old guy (greeter) saw me with my kids & was like where is their dad? He was so crusty, we were like really perv?

- I have a creeper at my mom's church . . . the creepy greeter freaks me out. I don't even like going to her church now.

- When you randomly get signed up to be a greeter for your church mass? #IhateChurch

- If a Wal-Mart greeter is warmer and more authentic than ones at church there is a problem.

- Today my greeter at Church told me to suck it up and stop complaining about being sore.

- "Nice to meet you. Who the hell are you?" Greeter at church this morning.

- That awkward moment when you're holding hands with your dad walking into church & the greeter tells you what a good looking couple you make.

- I would not join your church if the greeter gave me a flyer to another church and told me I should check them out next week.

- The greeter at church asked me how old I was and I told him I was 21. #mybirthdaybetterhurryup

- Just remembered a greeter at church slipped me a note with his number in it. I guess I have to be polite…call & let him down easy.

- The church greeter told me I looked sexy this morning. #awkward

- That awkward moment then the 80 year old greeter at church says "you'd be nice to cuddle with for a while" while hugging you. #mylife

Why bother?

Some churches I've consulted with cannot seem to recruit enough volunteers. People drop out after one or two weeks, some don't ever want to do it again, and some churches haven't even started a greeting ministry yet. I hear:

- I can't find anyone to do it.
- There are not enough volunteers.
- I don't know how to talk to a visitor.
- Getting volunteers to take the plunge.
- We don't do it because it's everyone's job.
- People say yes, but don't show up for duty.
- I'm afraid that we will mess up God's work in someone's life.

With all the challenges to recruiting and training greeters, we come to the question of why bother? Why put up with the organizational efforts and human resources it takes to manage such a challenge? Why spend hours of volunteer effort and energy to recruit, train, and equip greeters?

It's not enough to say "we've always done it this way." In the last two churches I served, the ministry of greeters was an operating assumption. One cannot keep programs in perpetuity simply because you have been doing them. Churches should know why they have such programs and why they should continue to invest hours of energy in recruiting, training, and developing a greeting ministry.

Why bother?

> *No church intends to give a visitor or member a bad experience, to leave them with feelings of being unwanted or unwelcomed. No church wants to be rude and hinder a family's journey of faith to Christ.*

Greeters are the servant volunteers who prepare the way for your guests and visitors to experience the presence of God in your worship service, to hear the Word of God proclaimed, and possibly to experience the renewing work of the Holy Spirit. I think the prophecy of John the Baptist preparing the way for Jesus is easily applied in the local church setting (Mark 1:3).

> *"The voice of one crying in the wilderness: 'Prepare the way of the Lord; Make His paths straight.'"*

Remember that the ministry of greeter exists to help others know and experience Jesus!

Greeters Notice People.

Greeters notice people. They are the first face of your church to its members and first time visitors. Greeters speak the language of kindness. Greeters help the bewildered walking in the hallways to find the right classroom or worship space. Greeters can set the atmosphere for people to experience the wonder of God's presence and the power of God's preached word.

Greeters serve a powerful role, even if that role is not immediately recognized and honored. The goal of their work is not conversion, but simply to be friendly faces, those who are there to meet practical needs of the moment. The lack of a hello from an unobservant greeter can have a long range impact, but a good welcome can prepare the way for more blessings.

The potential long reach of a hello.

My website (EvangelismCoach.org) has stories of the generational impact of the lack of hospitality from churches. Here is one from a family who dropped out of church over 40 years ago because no one said hello:

> *Over a good meal one night, an irreligious married couple and I spoke of church life, faith, Christ, and other topics. They both attended church 3 times a week growing up, but once they married and relocated to another city, they quit going.*
>
> *They hadn't been to church regularly for nearly 40 years and faith is no longer important to them. Their children weren't church goers and grew up without any real knowledge of the grace of God.*
>
> *I asked, "Why did you stop going?"*
>
> *"When we were newly married," they replied, "we relocated hundreds of miles away from our home town, away from family, friends, and our support network.*
>
> *"We visited a few churches of our brand and not one person said hello or took interest in us."*

Did you catch that? A generation of children grew up into adulthood in a non-Christian household because the parents couldn't find a church where they felt welcomed. One child became a Christian later in life, thanks to the saving grace of Christ.

The absent hello could very well have been a surface excuse for a deeper reason that the person chose not to reveal. But for that story to be given as the reason for dropping out of church suggests there was some painful truth to that experience.

Breaking a Broken Reed.

I received this email earlier this week, though I changed the details to remove church names and details to make it more generic. This could be true of many churches in the United States.

> *This morning I heard an account from a person who recently visited one of our churches. The person has chosen to get more involved with our denomination and has decided to go to a church somewhat close to where they live (praise God!). After two visits this person wanted to share with me the outcome of visiting the same church two weeks in a row. They thought I would be interested in their observation, and I certainly was.*

> *In two weeks of visiting no one greeted them, not even the pastor. No one ever handed them a bulletin, thanked them for coming, much less offered them an opportunity to enter their name and address in a pew attendance guest book. "Hello, we are glad to see you!" was clearly not in the DNA of this congregation with respect to visitors.*

In the second visit, the person decided to approach one of the [leaders] to see what the church might have to 'offer' should they make it their church home. The response was - "NOTHING. We have nothing to offer you." Ouch! This wasn't a huge church so it would be most obvious that someone was new.

A few weeks after I received that email, I actually met the person involved. She had dropped out of church for a few years, having been hurt in a horrible situation. She was coming back to the faith, exploring churches with great caution and attentiveness. Such an experience hurt her already broken spirit yet further.

Greeting Experiences are publically shared.

People share stories about church visiting experiences on the internet. Painful examples can be easily found. People will broadcast their experiences on sites like Facebook and Twitter without much thought or shame.

Church visitors comment on no-one saying hello, or too many people saying hello and seeming insincere. Here is one story I found online:

Not long ago we visited a certain church. Arriving on time, my wife I started walking past a fellow who seemed to be standing idly in the foyer. He stopped us and fairly demanded to know who we were and where we were from. Eventually I understood that this man with his ill-fitting sports coat and checkered shirt was the official church greeter of the day and that this was his way of welcoming visitors.

At about that time he extended his right hand which included two
or three half-inch scabs which I was obligated to grasp and shake .
. .

Imagine my thoughts when I was once welcomed in another church
by a very old-looking and overweight saint, wearing outdated
clothing and who was missing several teeth?

It seems that people expect to be greeted at a church, even if they are not Christian believers. Your greeters are part of your first impression team, whether for good or ill. People notice greeters.

Greeters have more impact than they think.

Greeters serve in quiet but vital roles. They make sure the church is ready for the service. They make sure to greet members and visitors and all the children as they arrive. Ushers help people to their seat and answer last minute questions that visitors may have.

Greeters and ushers may continue to serve during the worship service, helping the latecomers get situated, or even ministering to those who may have quietly stepped out into the hall to find some space.

As people leave the worship experience, greeters are there to give a final greeting and an invitation to return again.

First impressions are not about right doctrine, but about the emotional and relational experiences that people with your congregation.

Paige Lanier Chargois (34) gives a list of benefits that a vital greeting ministry will accomplish. It won't guarantee you hordes of new visitors, but an effective greeting ministry will

- Significantly affect visitor impressions

- Help to transform visitors into members
- Increase the perceived warmth of your congregation
- Raise the level of excellence expected in your ministries
- Enable members to move beyond themselves into outreach
- Instill pride and increase friendliness even among members
- Deepen the overall quality of hospitality in your congregation
- Help members derive blessings and benefits as much as visitors
- Provide perhaps the only opportunity for a family to minister together
- Change the concept of hospitality from food centered to outreach and care

Greeters demonstrate kindness.

Greeters take the initiative to demonstrate kindness in practical ways. This makes a lasting impression. Greeters are called to be kind, whoever the "other" person may be.

I once read that 75% of people feel anxiety / discomfort when entering a new space for the very first time as a total stranger. That suggests your first time guest may have a slightly elevated stress level and perhaps a narrowed focus as they try to get oriented to their surroundings. They might be wondering – where is everything? Where is the sanctuary? Where are the bathrooms?

Your greeting ministry can help take away that anxiety. Smiles and warm hospitality help alleviate some of those feelings. Taking the initiative to notice first time visitors, to greet them, welcome them, and talk to them can help soften the edge that people feel when going to a brand new place.

Help your guests find the sanctuary. Some older church buildings are not physically laid out very well. A greeter that personally guides the visitor to the sanctuary will relieve some of that spatial anxiety. I've been in a few places where getting to the sanctuary from the entry door is not obvious: *Walk down this hall, through that fellowship hall, and up the poorly lit stairwell. To avoid entering from behind the pulpit in the sanctuary, walk down that **left** hall so that you can enter the rear of the sanctuary.*

Help the bewildered. In 1996, I visited a huge church outside of Atlanta. I was lost and I was alone, trying to find the Sunday school class I wanted to attend. A greeter noticed my disorientation, approached me, and asked me a simple "Can I help you find what you are looking for?" I told her the class I was seeking, upon which she personally escorted me there.

That day I was the stranger. I didn't know my way around. I felt strange wandering the hall by myself. I was feeling pretty incompetent since I got lost. I have felt more comfortable navigating airport terminals than I felt in that church hallway.

Because she relieved the inner tension I felt, as a man, lost in strange building, I still remember her nearly 13 years later. I don't remember her name or her face, but I remember the experience of that church. This greeter's kindness helped me enjoy the rest of the morning.

Disarm the discomfort. At another recent dinner, a friend shared with me a story about a new family friend experiencing their church for the first time. After the worship service, the family friend noted that no one in the church said hello or even acknowledged her presence. She described how awkward, unwelcome, and very out of place she felt.

To the surprise of my friend, she mentioned that she'd return the following week, because my friend's son **took the initiative to say hello to her** after children's church was over.

Greet the Children. The kindness shown by greeting the children demonstrates that church is not just the world of adults. Some greeting teams prepare goodie bags of some kind for children: a coloring sheet, fresh crayons, or maybe even a gift or noiseless craft to assemble. Greeters who make the effort to greet the children personally as they come in will endear themselves to both parents and children.

Greeters notice people. Those who take the initiative to help the lost find their way offer an act of kindness that goes a long way to making and keeping a great impression of friendliness.

Greeters can help people connect.

Research shows that most people don't join a denomination, or even a church near to home—they join and connect where they bond with people. I've interviewed several people who still don't know the differences between the Presbyterians, Methodists and Episcopalians, but they like the people of the church they attend. Loyalty is with people, not so much an institution.

Your church growth is partially dependent on helping new people connect to your congregation. If your church desires to impact a person's life for the sake of the Gospel, your greeters help with that process. You can't impact people's lives if they don't come back to your church.

Potential Spiritual Impact. I received this note in my email. The writer is a high school friend and refers to events nearly 20 years ago when she was forced to go to church as a very troubled teenager. She reflects on influences that helped her come to her own faith in Christ as an adult.

> *It started with my parents forcing me into the car and forcing me out of the car every single Sunday. I sat on the back table and didn't participate or anything....really because I could NOT believe in something I couldn't see.*

> *Yet there was this one guy who kept coming up, every single week, to say hi, give me a hug, etc.....and even though I thought it was strange, I thought there must be something at work here...so I started listening more....then I actually started praying....then I actually started looking forward to the youth group and the fellowship with my peers.*

> *Then I started seeing people who really believed and were not only believers, but were willing to share, no matter how long it took, with someone totally outside the sphere of believers....totally awesome.....so.......thank you.*

Did you notice the power of a greeter in her story and journey to faith? She experienced a greeting and kindness that eventually influenced her into finding faith in Christ.

Action Steps – Chapter 2

1. Visit a church outside your denominational tradition. Visit one you've never been to before. Pay attention to your emotions as you enter the building. If they have greeters, how do they help or not help you? How did you feel with what help was provided?

2. Think of a time when you were the stranger in a new place. What helped you grow comfortable in that new environment?

3. Ask a few of your non-Christian friends to visit your church as an experiment. Offer them a cup of coffee or a lunch to tell you how they experienced your greeting ministry. Get their honest feedback.

4. What do your observations from questions 1-3 suggest about your greeting ministry and what your church might need to do to improve?

5. Share an awkward greeting experience you have had. Be respectful and leave names out.

6. Share an awesome greeting experience you have had. What made it great?

Chapter 3.

Organizing Your Church's Greeting Ministry

Some of the most creative ideas emerge from the swirl of chaos - Unknown

As the role of the church greeter has become a specialized ministry in most churches, you will need to organize it to make it run well.

Organization does not happen on its own. You might think that greeting is everyone's job, but nearly every group I encounter has experienced the failure of that claim. To say everyone is responsible ultimately means no one is responsible. The stories in the last chapter give some evidence of what happens when churches believe that everyone pays attention to the greeting process. It begins to fail.

Churches are social organisms. As they become more complex, they require more processes and clearly developed expectations. Then comes some need for consistency of experience, training for the volunteers, and a group of passionate people leading the ministry making sure the work gets done with excellence.

You might be at the place where you are just starting a greeting ministry. Since 2007, I've talked with several ministry leaders who are just beginning to organize a greeter program—it is a new concept in their church. Others seek to revitalize a greeting ministry that has been neglected. Still others are in a period with an interim pastor for a time of healing, recovery, and/or a launch into a new phase of growth when a new pastor comes.

You might be at the place where you realize that you need to organize and grow your current greeting ministry. You might have realized that your church is increasing in attendance numbers to the point where friendly greetings don't happen naturally anymore (like it did when you were an 18-member church).

Volunteer leaders do not want to put too much thought into how to re-invent the organizational wheel. Therefore, they search the Internet. People find their way to EvangelismCoach.org seeking how to organize a greeter ministry or how to provide training for greeters. I created ChurchGreeterTraining.com in response to that need.

I want to lay out some ideas and models for organizing your greeting ministry. But before we get into practical organizational structures, let's take some pages to define some organizational observations or principles.

Let common sense prevail. Some organizational structure is necessary. However, too much organization will burden any kind of program. No organizational structure for your greeting ministry needs to be so rigid as to squash personal initiative, nor so loose that nothing gets accomplished. The human tendency is either to over-organize or under-organize.

As you develop your custom training material, remember, you will not be writing an employee manual, nor setting so many nitpicky policies that your volunteers can't remember all the rules. You are developing guidelines towards excellence.

Many variables. There are so many variables that come into play when considering how to organize your greeting ministry and train people for it. For example:

- The number of people attending your worship services.
- The number of entry points to your facilities.
- The number of worship services.
- The number of related services such as childcare, hospitality centers, and Sunday school.

It can get even more complex for multi-site campuses and parking lot ministries. All of these variables come into play when determining the shape, scalability, and scope of your greeting ministry.

Adapt these observations to your context. What follows are a couple of suggestions. Develop what works for your congregation's size and setting. Figure out a model that works in your church, but don't make the mistake of over-organizing it. Each church has its own cultural context and must adapt all processes to its local situation. What may work in one town, may not work in another.

We've all likely learned over the years that we can't hit the green button on spiritual photocopier and make a duplicate image of someone else's organization in our church. We need to see the principles, and then contextualize them for our local situation. Greeter ministry is a loose team of volunteers who gather to complete the task of giving visitors and members a warm welcome. Keep your structure as simple as possible to get the ministry well done. The names of roles below are simply conventions to describe a function. You can choose your own terms.

Behind the scenes: Administrative Leadership

Coordinator. This person oversees the process of recruiting and training greeters and may serve as the central contact person to the church's leadership board or hospitality committee to which they are accountable. This is the key contact person for this entire specialized ministry.

In general, this ministry coordinator sees that the greeting ministry is carried out effectively during church services and special events. The coordinator has liberty to walk the hallways of the church to make sure the greeting ministry is running well and troubleshoot any points of difficulty.

This person also develops the training program for greeters and oversees obtaining administrative supplies such as name badges, developing checklists and coaching new greeters.

The coordinator might naturally notice people who love to greet and take the initiative to invite them to volunteer.

The coordinator may maintain a list of people who agree to serve as back-up when the scheduled greeter is unable to serve.

Some churches are large enough where this is an actual staff position. Others might set this as a rotating position with a term limit (e.g., 1 year, 3 years), or let an effective volunteer who loves this work to keep running it, with the requirement for that person to train a replacement for when the day comes to turn the leadership over to the next leader.

Churches might invest in this person's ongoing training in the whole realm of hospitality ministry and volunteer recruitment by budgeting funds for training resources and conferences and online seminars.

Recruiter. Sometimes additional volunteers will focus on recruitment of greeters for the worship services -- the human resourcing side of the greeting ministry. Others will have this included in the role of the greeting coordinator.

This may be a shorter volunteer commitment like three or six months.

This person needs some administrative gifting to organize the recruitment of volunteers, the schedules of volunteers, training meetings, and volunteer appreciation ceremonies. It is helpful for this person to be comfortable with cold call recruiting efforts to members of the church, as well of course, with personal face to face recruitment.

This person may also give reminders when people are scheduled to serve, by calling or emailing greeters the Wednesday before their scheduled Sunday, for example. This person may handle the scheduling of backup greeters when necessary.

Communicating a word of thanks when people rotate off is also a key task of the recruiter. Your greeters are your front line volunteers! Love them and appreciate them.

Hospitality Committee. Some churches are large enough to have a committee or group that manages all hospitality functions of the church and its various events, not just greeting at principal worship services. They oversee the entire area of hospitality: first impressions, greeting, welcome, after service reception, visitor follow-up and assimilation.

This committee looks at the church's calendar to make sure that special events such as annual celebrations, block parties, or church homecomings, for example, are covered by the hospitality ministry.

It takes care of the <u>administrative side</u> of the hospitality ministry. However you choose to call it, this committee must be empowered to get things done.

One church I spoke with uses this committee to make sure that all church events on the calendar have greeters, ushers, and parking lot attendants. Their role was simply administrative. Members of this committee formed teams with responsibility in specialized areas: one focused on greeters and ushers, another on the parking lot, and another on building maintenance and presentation / custodial issues.

The Front Line Volunteers—The Greeters

Depending on the size of your church and the number of services and entry points, volunteer teams are typically broken down into the following designations based on ministry area and range of responsibility.

Some of these teams may have their own captains, recruiters, or organizers as subsets of the hospitality team described above. Terms like "Head Greeter" or "Lead Usher" or "Team Captain" are part of the organizational structure to facilitate communication and cooperation as your teams require more specialization due to your church's growth.

Just remember – don't over-organize.

You may choose to organize in such a way that duties overlap for the sake of multi-tasking. Some duties may not be useful in smaller churches. Some overlapping of duties may not be helpful in larger churches. In smaller churches, ushers and greeters may very well be the same people. In larger churches, there may be more specialization of duties.

This isn't a duty list—that comes in a later chapter—but is intended to be enough of a description to help you consider the various places volunteer greeters can serve.

Door Greeters. Door greeters are usually the first smiling face people see as they enter through the door. Most conversations are brief because the flow of people entering the church before worship and the flow of people exiting the building after worship is generally steady, even heavy. Conversations cannot be long because there is no time for it.

A smile, eye contact, and a handshake are typical forms of North American greeting. Note, a growing number of people are concerned about germs and may choose not to do participate in a handshake. Others may go beyond the handshake and offer to give hugs when appropriate.

Some churches recruit entire families to serve at one of the entry doors, as opposed to a solo greeter.

Pay attention to the diversity of your greeters to make sure they represent the diversity of your congregation and your community.

Hospitality / Visitor Center / Welcome Desk. This team manages the table where information about the various programs of your church is available. This is an ideal visitor connection point because longer conversations are possible, particularly with newcomers to the church. If you have visitor welcome packets to distribute, for example, your volunteers are on hand to share them in a meaningful way.

Some churches will double up this visitor center with that of an information or reception desk, where church members can sign up as volunteers for events, submit address changes, trade messages, or check the church calendar. In my experience, multi-purposing this table / center tends to get so crowded that visitors you are trying to greet may never get to the table to get their visitor packet or marketing giveaway.

Guides. These specialized team members have the liberty to leave the hospitality center or front door to escort people to other parts of the building such as the nursery, the Christian education wing, the bookstore, or directly to the sanctuary. It was this type of person who rescued me in that Atlanta church.

In planning for the number of guides you will need, remember the obvious fact that when a guide takes a visitor directly to a specific destination, that leaves your front door or hospitality center down one guide!

During the walking time, guides can naturally provide much more personal interaction than an entry door greeter or the staff of the hospitality center.

Ushers. These volunteers are stationed near the sanctuary or auditorium doors. They guide people to available seating and answer last minute questions. During worship, they receive the offering and manage issues of decorum.

As mentioned, the ministry of usher has developed a specialization that is a little different than the function of church greeters.

Yet, they still play an important role in greeting people as they are led to their seats prior to the service. See Chapter Seven for more on ushers.

Parking Lot Teams. Some campuses have to manage the traffic in their parking lots. These parking lot teams serve to guide people to available parking and help traffic flow during the times between the services.

In one church I served, our front parking lot had only 18 spaces that we reserved for visitors and pastors, and those with disabilities. Our regular attendees knew not to use that lot, but visitors got to use it. For special events where we knew we'd have lots of first time visitors, we used a parking lot greeter to help people find the rear parking lot and then attendants to help point out the obscure entry door. We knew we'd need every available space in the front lot for handicapped parking.

In larger parking lots, some churches use shuttles to help get people to the main building. Drivers of shuttles are part of that team.

Your parking lot teams might offer valet parking for those who need assistance. Others might be at the ready with an umbrella during wet weather or open the door for passengers being dropped off by taxi.

In a recent church I visited, the parking lot team quickly guided me to available parking, facilitating an easy entrance to the gathering place in the school gym. They said hello with a smile, setting an example for the experience to come.

Security. Some campuses have recently added security teams to the list. Members of this team watch the building, the parking lots, and wander the halls to be available if a crisis unfolds.

Teams may enlist off-duty police officers who are paid or volunteer, and some teams have medical personnel available, who can be contacted in case of medical emergency.

In one church we attended for two years, this team kept a careful eye on the empty seats during altar calls since purses and belongings were left on the seats. Security guards watched the parking lot to prevent theft or damage.

Layers of greeting.

This is a new term I'm seeing in the literature, particularly as more and more churches want to develop their hospitality ministry. It refers to the number of potential contact points that a visitor might experience when coming to your church for the first time. For example, visitors may potentially receive a:

- Greeting by parking lot staff at the entrance to the lot.
- Greeting by a volunteer who opens car doors for people.
- Greeting by the shuttle driver.
- Greeting by the front door greeter as people walk in.
- Guide who escorts visitors to the information booth where two or three people are available for extended conversation.
- Guide who leads visitors to the children's ministry area and back to the sanctuary.
- Hand off to the usher who greets visitors with the focus on today's service.
- Hand off to the church member next to whom the usher seats visitors who concludes the church's hospitality ministry up to the start of worship.

Each one of these points is another layer of greeting. Some churches may have so over-developed their greeting process that they have created a human wall. Depending on the size of your church, you'll have different layers of greeting already in place.

Greeting can be taken too far if your church visitor or member has to run through a human wall just to get to the sanctuary. I've read accounts from church visitors that felt overwhelmed with the human obstacles in their way that they needed to overcome just to arrive at their seats: parking lot attendants, escorts to the door, guides to the children's area, escorted here and there, nosy people presuming to ask personal questions, ushers asking the same questions that the foyer and parking lot greeters asked just moments before.

Take some time to evaluate your current process and see if you have too much. If so, fine tune it accordingly. You can think of it in terms of:

- Front lines: door greeters.
- Secondary line: guides and hospitality center volunteers.
- Third line: ushers.

How many greeters do you need?

There are multiple variables from campus size, number of entry points and how specialized you want your teams to be. Other variables include duration of volunteer service and how many layers of greeting you want to give.

There is no magic number. I can't tell you that a church of 400 needs 40 greeters, or that a church of 28 needs 2.

What is clear is that you want to avoid "*the human wall*" – so many layers of greeting and greeters that it seems too friendly or overwhelming, particularly for the first time visitor. You want to be sure your greeting is experienced as sincere and not as artificial friendliness.

If you are just starting out, be sure you have all your principal entry doors covered at every service as well as some ushers at the entrance to the sanctuary. Larger churches may decide that some doors like the main entry need more greeters than other doors off the back education wing, for example.

How many you need is up to you and the type of scheduling you plan to use. Start by counting the number of entry points to get a grasp of your needs.

At my first church, we only had one entry point at the end of a very long hall. We had one greeter at that door, and then one at the other end of the hall where they further directed visitors to the sanctuary. That last walk to the sanctuary was so short that there was no need to personally escort anyone.

How long do volunteers serve?

Some kind of rotation schedule for your volunteers is a tried and true practice. Determine what works best for your church.

Rotation models of one month at a time, or once a month, first Sunday of the month, for examples, ensure a limited time commitment. Others blend a rotation model with some slots given for those that have random schedules and can only serve every now and then. For instance, I might serve only once a month, but which Sunday is determined by my ministry travel schedule. I might be gone two or three Sundays a month, or none at all. You need to determine what works in the life of your congregation.

Rotation helps avoid burnout of your volunteers. Greeting is often a one way giving process without expectation of a return. Rotating out gives people the chance to recharge personal batteries.

I prefer asking people for a one month commitment when they serve as door greeters. This can help them get to know members, recognize faces quickly, and have the potential to spot a first time visitor without having to ask. But, I realize with busy lives, and in some churches, multiple obligations, this may not work for many.

Some may choose to ask people to serve for 6-8 weeks or even a quarter. It's a matter of finding what works for your ministry context, and how well volunteers love to serve in the ministry of greeting. The next chapter provides helpful guidelines for recruiting volunteers.

Action Steps – Chapter 3:

1. Take a few moments and map out some possible structures to your greeting ministry.

2. Count the number of entry doors to your facilities.

3. Count the number of entry points to your sanctuary.

4. Count how many services you have in a weekend.

5. How many layers of greeting do you have right now? Do you have too many? Not enough? Do you need to make adjustments?

6. Decide upon the layers of greeting you want to develop. For example, do you want front door greeters as well as ushers at the entrances of the sanctuary? Do you want parking lot attendants? Do you have a hospitality center that needs to be staffed?

7. Evaluate and decide how to schedule your greeters and which kind of rotation fits your needs. Discover how the scheduling system currently functions, and speak with the recruiter or coordinator to see how it is working.

Chapter 4.

Recruiting Volunteer Greeters

I love my church!! Every Sunday walking in I'm greeted with a smile from all our wonderful greeters and ushers. Thank you! — Twitter User

Greeting teams run on the efforts of volunteers in your church. They are the ones who help form the first impression your members and guests will have on that given Sunday.

You may use spiritual gift inventories to help place people in ministries related to their gifts and passions. This helps you locate people who might have the gift mix you are looking for in greeting.

You may require new greeters to be church members or have attended a new member class before they can volunteer. Others may decide that since greeters are to reflect the very welcome of the Lord, they need to know Jesus as their Savior so they may show His grace as they greet your members and prospective members. Still others might decide that the ministry of greeting is a good volunteer entry point for those who are not yet believers but seem to be growing towards Christ.

As they serve in greeting ministry, they experience the Kingdom values they learn about. These are matters for your local church to determine.

For this chapter, I assume you are actively recruiting a team of volunteers who serve, and you are empowered to make things happen. I'm not addressing the development of your hospitality committee or any other administrative leadership.

If you are in charge of recruiting greeters, here is a possible strategy. Customize for your own context.

- Map out the positions that need to be filled.
- Determine how many greeters you will need (plus on-call backups).
- Brainstorm names of potential recruits. Think of people who naturally do this, and who are not already over-committed to other ministry areas.
- Recruit them personally.
- When all else fails, start making bulletin announcements and cold calls.

What if we can't get any volunteers for greeter ministry?

Several readers of my website have asked me this question:

> Our church doesn't have enough people who are interested in being greeters. We can't get any volunteers. Any ideas?

Another one put it this way:

How would you answer the comment "we don't need a greeter program...we are all 'on duty' and are already greeting the visitors". ..."we don't need to have a formalized program or have someone tell us how to greet?"

The lack of people interested in greeters and hospitality ministry is a problem in many churches. This attitude can abide in a small church where everyone believes that everyone greets each other. Every Sunday, members of this small church are warmly greeted and engaged in conversation with other church members that they do not even see the presence of visitors. Since many church members are so well connected and emotionally engaged, they might assume visitors will get themselves connected. This is simply a blind spot. Greeting and welcoming people into your Christian fellowship need to be deliberate and well-planned efforts or they will fall well short of your expectations. More importantly, your congregation will fail in adequately reflecting the light of Jesus.

Likewise, this volunteer apathy occurs in declining churches that are so set in their ways that they have lost the vision for reaching newcomers. I've visited churches whose members could care less about accommodating visitors with things like helpful signage or a warm hello. Members of such churches do not see the value in this aspect of hospitality ministry. They have become inward focused and have forgotten the vision of reaching out to new people with the Gospel of Jesus.

The problem behind this attitude is a lack of vision. The vision for hospitality ministry must be regularly lifted up and repeated for hospitality ministry to become a value of your church. Your members must see your visitors differently. Your visitors are your guests and a gift of God. They are men, women, and children whom the Holy Spirit brings to your church for a reason: Kingdom impact.

Many visitors are already believers and followers of Christ. They look for a place where they can serve, use their gifts and talents, and participate in the life and mission of the church to bless its community. Other visitors might be on their journey to discover Christ. Whether they are intentionally seeking Him because of a pressing felt need, or simply responding to ongoing invitations of your church members, or even choosing to come because of your church's mission, when they visit your church, do they experience the Good News both in word and in action?

Hospitality ministries help your church visitors decide to return. Hospitality ministries help your guests organically develop new relationships within your congregation. Good hospitality practices seek to honor your church visitors as valued guests, not as intruders. Without the honoring of your guests through awesome red carpet hospitality, your church will not fulfill its vision of transforming lives for Jesus Christ.

When you recruit volunteers, some will not understand their importance in the welcome mission of your church. They will **do a job** versus **serve a ministry**. These are the volunteers who won't show up, won't really care, and won't find a last minute replacement. It falls on you to recruit, cast vision, and provide regular training to prevent that attitude from happening.

You'll need to remind your volunteers regularly about the importance of the work they do. Share stories with them of families who get involved in your church because of a great welcome they received.

And then, don't forget to say thank you. Find ways to say thanks in a manner that your volunteers will receive. Some like public thanks, others prefer to be thanked in private.

If you cannot find willing greeters, you'll need to start working on vision casting for hospitality ministries. Connect that hospitality vision to the ministry of your church. Take time over the next few months to plan how you will start to achieve that.

How many greeters do you need?

As I mentioned in the previous chapter, it is impossible to dictate to you the exact number of greeters you will need due to the many variables of your context.

If you've gone through the action steps in the previous chapter to identify potential greeters, you'll want to add to that list a number of back up substitutes to fill the role in a pinch. These are people who don't want to serve as greeters regularly, but are possibly available to serve in a last minute schedule change. They would be "on-call" as needed.

Greeting teams need to reflect the demographic make-up of the congregation. Resist calling only on the extroverts, to whom greeting comes naturally. Make it a goal for your greeting team to represent more than just one social status, gender, or even age. Use families and singles, the widowed, the divorced, immigrants and citizens. Mix it up so that your greeter team reflects the diversity of your congregation. As long as your volunteers can smile and greet, they can serve well, even if they need a little training.

Who to look for

> *I was asked by a 6 yr old in church today if I was new. When I said I was, her response: "Well, I hope you feel very welcome here." – Twitter User*

In my last congregation in Richmond, there was a gentleman who was always greeting visitors and always bringing visitors. He seemed to be introducing people on Sundays and making sure they had their practical needs met—Sunday in and Sunday out. He was a natural greeter. He started serving at the entry door to our church in order to greet everyone walking in the door. To serve on the team as a regular greeter was a cinch for him. He was an obvious one to recruit for the team.

If you are just starting to identify greeters for your organized greeting team, start with the "easy ones." As you do further recruiting, you want people who love this ministry. Look for a level of spiritual maturity. If you choose to use greeters who are not yet believers, look for those who still model Kingdom values and are growing towards faith in Jesus. Set some standards and challenge people to reach for them. Look for those who show natural warmth towards people, particularly your visitors. Look for those whose mindset is clearly "other oriented." Keep in mind that not everyone who offers to help is easily able to make the shift in orientation away from self to others. Many of us are stuck in our infant stage of *me first*.

Next, pray about those members who show potential in this ministry. Greeters can be trained. I would suggest that you don't <u>only</u> recruit those who have proven themselves as leaders in your congregation. Search for those whom you think have potential as well. This will help you train up future leaders, perhaps train your replacement, and spread the joy of ministry around. Finally, this helps you avoid overloading existing congregational leaders.

> *Church Greeters who scowl when they are told good morning really need to evaluate their spiritual gifts. -- Twitter User*

People of Good Character

Recruit men, women, children and families of good character and reputation. Visitors may know your greeters from seeing them around town. Visitors might form an impression of your church based on where your greeter was seen a few days before. I can't tell you how many laypeople have told me how important that is. In small towns, this may be more important than in larger cities where anonymity is more achievable.

> *From rock 'n roller to church door greeter in less than 12 hours. Sometimes I feel like I lead a double life. – Twitter User*

You'll want people who have a history of showing kindness and whose friendliness seems natural. You'll also want to consider your observations of a person's hygiene habits. You might quickly rule out a few people.

Consider that greeters in the parking lot and those assigned to security may need particular training and skills.

How to Recruit Volunteers

Look through the upcoming Chapter 6 on the character of a greeter. This will also give you some guidance on the type of people you will be looking for. If your church uses spiritual gifts inventories as part of the ministry, look for those who have the gift mix of a greeter.

After identifying your initial list of greeters, the following two steps will give you a pool of volunteers to establish your team.

Personal recruitment

Smaller churches may want to focus on personal recruitment rather than relying on bulletins and newsletters. From my own experience, plus conversations I've had with coordinators, impersonal announcements don't work as effectively as personal contact, a face to face invitation to become a greeter.

Greeting coordinators in larger churches, though constrained by time perhaps, can easily supplement existing recruiting channels with the personal invitation to those who show potential.

The first step in personal recruitment is to notice people personally who have a natural passion for saying hello. Look for ones who take the initiative to meet the stranger, the ones who always seem to approach people, or the ones who seem to find small talk easy – these are the easiest greeters to recruit.

The second step for personal recruitment is to go beyond the "Sunday morning hallway hopeful ask." Instead of stopping a person in the hallway to make a recruiting pitch, offer to take them out for a cup of coffee, or host dessert at your house. Emphasize the importance of this ministry by avoiding the rush, by displaying the very welcome to them your greeting ministry is designed to provide.

Share some of the ministry vision of hospitality and greeting. Share your vision of what you hope the greeting ministry will be and how important you feel it is to the work of the overall ministry and the evangelistic vision of your church. You'll be able to communicate your passion as you talk about why you love this work of greeting the visitor and why you feel it is important. This obviously goes way beyond the typical hallway hopeful ask: "Can you be a greeter next week?"

During this kind of conversation, you can notice body language and verbal clues that tell you if your invitee is catching on to the vision. You can adjust your conversation as you need.

Once you have talked at length about this vision for ministry, it is time for the third step—the ask. "I want to invite you to consider joining our ministry team as a greeter. Would you like to take some time and pray about this role?"

Some people will say yes right away, others will appreciate the space to pray and consider their other obligations. Give them a call after a few days and ask them if they have decided yet.

During your conversation, you may detect a hesitation. That hesitation may reflect their anticipated worry and embarrassment over not knowing what to say or how to act. Make sure you mention that you offer training to help them grow in their skills and thus alleviate their worries. This will help the potentially nervous greeter get on board with your work by answering an unspoken objection that is likely there. I share more about training topics and ideas in the next chapter.

When you randomly get signed up to be a greeter for your church mass? #ihatechurch – Twitter User

Broad and General Recruitment

Bulletins, Announcements, Newsletters. These are typical advertising channels to solicit volunteers. Your challenge is to write announcements that don't seem like begging, and to communicate its importance in such a little space.

Ask your pastor for the occasional reminder. There is a select group of people in your congregation that will only listen to the pastor's appeal. As much as we might wish it were different, this is a reality. Every now and then, the pastor should lift up the value of the welcoming process and the role that greeters play in the process and remind people of the simple next step they can take in their discipleship by participating in the welcome ministry.

Cold Calling. One recruiter simply picked up the church phone directory and started cold calling people, asking them to commit to greeting for a month. If there was hesitancy, she'd ask for one Sunday out of the month instead of the whole month. This recruiter found that Sunday afternoon, after people had returned home from the morning service, was the best time for her to make these cold calls.

Have your existing greeters help recruit new people. Empower your current greeters to find new people to serve alongside them. Encourage them to look at their friends in church and invite them to serve with them on a given Sunday. As a ministry coordinator, you may want to offer them help in how to recruit. You may think it is easy, but some of our volunteers get nervous at the thought of recruiting.

Ask people to serve for a limited time period. Some people might avoid the greeter role out of the fear that they'll be stuck doing that job for the rest of their volunteer life. Perhaps you have known people who were asked to fill in for a sick greeter and found themselves still in that role 7 years later.

Recruit volunteers who want to step into some sort of ministry. Seek out the college-aged, newly graduated, and young married couples, those between 19 and their mid-30s. Sometimes, these groups can feel marginalized from the congregation. They tend to respond very well to personal requests for greater involvement.

Some members respond "not now." Make a note beside those names. Their schedule may not permit because of travel or some other obligation.

Some will say "No" or "That's not my thing." Don't insist on making them do it. You want joyful people who are happily serving as your greeters. One recruiter told me that one of the church board members actually said "I don't want to make new friends." This person should not be on the greeting team!

One church does things a little differently. They hold pre-service gatherings for volunteers on Sunday mornings prior to the service. Here is what their pastor wrote about how they choose greeters that Sunday.

We want to make sure the friendliest people with the most genuine smiles are stationed as greeters. To choose our greeters, we have been known to do smile practice in our pre-service volunteer meeting. Not only does everyone get to practice putting on a huge smile, but the ones who end up as greeters understand that the smile they give guests is so important that their own smiles just landed them the position! There's an old business axiom that says

you can hire unfriendly people and work hard to teach them to

smile or you can hire smiling friendly people and turn them loose.

The latter seems like a nice shortcut to us, which is why we think

it's important to specifically choose our greeters instead of simply

taking the first volunteers for that position (Searcy, Fusion, 57).

Reminding greeters

It has been a good practice of many recruiters to send written reminders to greeters a week before their rotation is to start. You might send a reminder email, a hand written note, or a personal phone call (but not a voice mail). These reminders can include the when and where, a hospitality ministry tip, or how many Sundays they are serving. It could also be a series of emails you send.

You are free to use any of the greeting tips found in the Greeter Category or Hospitality Category at Evangelismcoach.org, as long as you include a link and the title of the article.

You could also invite feedback on their last experience, or invite questions to come back to you via email, text messaging, or even in the personal phone calls. This may offer you the opportunity to troubleshoot potential problems.

Thanking greeters

Don't forget to thank your greeters when their rotation is over. You might want to send a hand written thank you note, or some other token of appreciation. A word of thanks goes a long way in keeping your volunteers for future work.

People want to be noticed and appreciated for their contributions. The sense of personal accomplishment one feels when making an impact on a person's morning can be motivating, but it is much more so when someone notices the good ministry and attaches worth to it.

Don't take your greeters for granted. Love on them and affirm them when they serve. Listen for those who tell you how much they enjoyed the experience of greeting. You'll want to use them again. Watch or listen for stories of helpful greeters and use those stories as positive examples in future training meetings.

Use a Vision Refresh Meeting as a starting point

A good time to recruit greeters is in the few weeks leading up to a meeting focused on refreshing the vision for church hospitality. During this meeting, you can provide training using the material I provide for you in the next chapter.

It may have been a long time since you held a training meeting for greeters, or your church may not have had one in the last decade since the last volunteer retired. You may encounter a common attitude held by some volunteers, who dismiss a training meeting with "I don't need training to say hello. I know what I'm doing."

To counter that objection, reframe this meeting as a vision meeting for greeters and all church hospitality workers, and sneak in some training while you are at it. One hospitality ministry leader I talk with on occasion holds these meetings three times a year. She uses this connection point to introduce new greeters, and provide ongoing training for the hospitality ministry.

The vision gathering is a great connection point to welcome new greeters, tell stories of new members who felt welcomed, say thank you in public ways, troubleshoot any problems, and provide a chance to once again reinforce the value of your hospitality ministry. This meeting also gives you a recruitment tool in your conversations with potentially nervous greeters who remain unsure as to their participation in this ministry.

Action steps – Chapter 4

1. Who is in charge of the greeter recruitment?

2. What kind of scheduling will you use?

3. What gift mix do you think is needed in your greeter recruits?

4. What tools can you develop to help your recruiter get the work done?

5. Brainstorm names of people you think you'd like to recruit. Use this coming weekend to watch for those who might make good greeters.

6. What additional steps would you take in recruiting greeters?

7. Ask those who have recruited before you what they found helpful in doing to recruit greeters. Add that to your list of what works in your congregation.

8. Who are your current greeters? What can you do this week to say "Thank You" to them?

9. If you love greeting ministry, write down 3 reasons this ministry brings your joy. How can these reasons influence your conversation with potentially new greeters?

Chapter 5.

Training For Your Church Greeters

I'm going to be a greeter for the first time at church today. A little nervous, hope it goes smooth (Twitter User)

I have a friend who was called Saturday night to be a greeter on Sunday morning. She agreed to serve in a new role. She had never been a greeter before. After hanging up the phone, a sense of anxiety began to rise up. What was she supposed to do? What would she say? What was she to wear the next morning? Where was she supposed to stand?

To complicate matters further, there had been a tragic accident in the church building the night before. A church member had died in a freak accident in the sanctuary. My friend found herself in a very uncomfortable situation. Listen to her questions / comments:

- I did not want to say no, I wanted to serve.
- I instantly felt nervous — would I mess up?
- Would I embarrass myself, or my church, or the church visitor?
- I couldn't rest well that night, because I was nervous and wanted to do a good job.

- What would I say to the group of 200 people walking in through the door?

Your volunteers want to do their ministry right. If they have never served as greeters before, they may be nervous about failing, of not pleasing you as their leader, and maybe quietly fearful that you might ask too much of them.

Not everyone is an extrovert—not everyone finds it easy to greet strangers or initiate small talk. Some newly recruited greeters may not know what to say while they stand at the door and shake hands. It might be a little embarrassing for them to tell you "I don't know how to do this."

Do they know what a greeter does?

In the current demographic makeup of our new church development, the majority of our church attendees are:

- Recently re-churched after years and years away.
- New believers Christ.
- Not yet Christians, but are exploring faith with our community.

Many have not been in church since they attended as children—10, 20 or even 30 years ago. The question was obvious to us: "Do any of them know what a greeter is or does?"

As our leadership team started to list potential volunteers to ask, we saw the need for one of us to disciple new greeters in the art of welcoming people to our congregation.

Help your new greeters feel more confident.

Providing new greeters clear guidelines and direction, as well as sample things to say goes a long way in helping them to feel less nervous about serving.

Training helps alleviate much of the awkwardness that new greeters might experience. Training gives them a forum to raise questions and prepare them for the work at hand, and even role play situations. Ongoing training helps you show them the importance and impact of their ministry. Training gives you the opportunity to make clear your expectations.

Don't assume your new greeters know what you expect of them. Evidence from the search logs of EvangelismCoach.org and some informal poll data suggests that greeters want training. They ask Google:

- What do I say as a greeter?
- What do I wear as a church greeter?
- How do I serve as a greeter?
- What does a greeter do?

Providing training opportunities may relieve the nervousness in some of your new volunteers if your service is tightly ordered and highly liturgical. A Catholic Mass or an Episcopal liturgy, or a traditionally formal Protestant worship service carries a certain level of formality, proper order and sense of decorum. In a formal procession, ushers may have particular places to walk at particular times. They may be expected to pass the offering plates in a synchronous fashion. Greeters may feel nervous at potentially disturbing the sacredness of the worship space.

Don't just stop with one meeting. Ongoing training will allow you to keep the motivation and quality high. As you plan training sessions with your greeters, keep your ultimate focus on <u>doing ministry</u>, not just the mechanics or process of doing ministry. An exclusive focus on the process and policies may lead to a mechanical and insincere attempt at hospitality. Focusing on the ministry will convey the genuine warmth and welcome befitting the service of welcoming others in the house of the Lord. As Paul wrote to the church at Colossae:

> *And whatever you do in word or deed, do everything in the name of the Lord Jesus, giving thanks to God the Father through him.*
> *Colossians 3:17*

Genuine and sincere

Greeting is noticing people. Effective greeting shows sincere interest. It demonstrates genuine concern and care for the visitors and members that God brings to your church.

Someone is quoted as having said, "If you can fake sincerity, you've got it made."[1] One can organize friendliness, but one cannot fake sincerity. Fake sincerity is as phony as a seven-dollar bill. Your greeters, ushers and the congregation all need to display genuine sincerity in their greeting. Visitors want to feel genuinely welcomed. Members want to feel important to your congregation. A mechanical greeting from a volunteer doesn't contribute to the experience you want your visitors to have.

---

[1] I've seen this quote attributed to actor George Burns, Groucho Marx, movie Producer Sam Goldwyn, and more recently the TV character Dr. House.

"There is only so many ways to say good morning." – Twitter User

An over-the-top greeting feels phony. I've walked into an ice cream shop and the staff starts to sing while still personalizing someone else's ice cream mixture on the counter. Or, the odd experience at fast food restaurants when the cashier yells out a welcome to you as you enter, while collecting money from a customer who has already been served. This multi-tasking does not make the hello seem very genuine. This practice might be a team builder for the franchise staff, but saying hello while mixing ice cream or preparing a taco doesn't convey a genuine greeting.

Likewise, the success of your greeting ministry is also connected to the overall relational warmth of the congregation. The greeters can be friendly, but if that initial, warm welcome is followed in the sanctuary by a congregation as emotionally cold as liquid nitrogen, well, you have a problem.

I have attended churches where I have experienced exactly that. I left with the impression that greeters were ones who cared, but the rest of the congregation didn't. You can train greeters, offer suggestions as to what to say, put them in the appropriate areas to conduct their ministry, but if there is no relational warmth from the congregation during the service, your greeting unfortunately may be perceived as empty insincere words and actions. Your greeting doesn't seem sincere and genuine when it masks the coldness of a congregation. Regular training allows you to remind people that they are never "off duty" from being friendly. The preacher can help the greeting ministry by regularly addressing the congregation as a whole about the joy of the Lord and the need to express it!

A science and an art

The success of greeting ministry is not exclusively on how well your training and your plans are executed. Those form only one part of the equation—the mechanical part, the "science" of greeting.

This is where the art comes in. This ministry is more than formality and church growth techniques and processes. Greeters may want to know what to do and what to say, but each one has to make sure their greeting is flavored with his or her own personality.

Many of us have likely experienced an apathetic check-out clerk, or the emotionally cold customer service representative reading a script. I have been welcomed by greeters absent-mindedly *doing their jobs*, rather than appearing glad that I was visiting their church.

You want your greeters to put their own personality into their ministry. While you establish specific boundaries and guidelines in training, encourage your greeters and ushers to take their own initiative by adding their own touch in saying hello.

Train the Heart

As you prepare your training, remember that you cannot cover every possible situation. Instead of a step by step how-to manual to give to your greeters, focus your training on the atmosphere you want to create. Invite your team to help you create the environment of hospitality that you want and you'll see the warmth of your hospitality and greeting go way up.

Focus on the principles and values of your hospitality ministry. Focus on the character of the greeter. Engage the heart. The details of implementation will follow.

Regularly Scheduled Training

A regular training meeting can increase your volunteer base by recasting a full vision of the importance of your hospitality ministry. The training session can be a great place to review and discuss the hospitality practices of your church. The training session helps your team through some of the mechanics of how to distribute a visitor packet or collect visitor contact information. For those churches that have more formal liturgy, a session can give you a place to help your ushers learn how to collect the offering.

Common questions about greeting can easily be addressed and compiled for future training. Schedule role playing into your training—a great way to learn how to greet people in the name of the Lord Jesus. Informing your greeters about the full breadth of ministries in your congregation equips them with knowledge to share with your visitors. Finally, the training meeting is also an ideal place to create community among your greeters.

How often should you hold training meetings? The simple answer is determined by the local context and size of your ministry. For example, the administrative committee may meet monthly or every two months to respond to needs, monitor developing situations and plans, and plan ahead for upcoming events, while training workshops for greeters and ushers may be annual or semi-annual, or as needed. Plan a minimum of 2-3 hours. Some books recommend a whole day.

If you are just starting a greeting ministry, 3-6 hours is a more likely time frame for your initial meeting. It really all depends on how much responsibility you are giving your greeters. In the sample workshop I've given you in Appendix C, 2-3 hours would be sufficient.

During your training meeting, make sure you give people time to interact in small group discussions. This will allow them to connect relationally, to teach themselves, and connect to your ministry values a little more personally.

A great practice Sunday morning before people begin to arrive is for the team to gather like a football team huddles before the next play. Here new greeters can be introduced. Last minute details can be handled. Bulletin concerns and special announcements to be made that day can be discussed. Most importantly, the team can take some time to quiet themselves before the Father to ask Him to still their own anxieties, and to fill them with the Holy Spirit to shine the light of Jesus before all they serve that day. Five minutes is all you need.

Some greeting teams schedule another short *huddle* directly after the service to debrief, that is, to celebrate what God did that day by sharing with each other personal encounters and to address immediate concerns that came up. Ordinarily, the team captain or head greeter moderates the discussion, highlighting best practices and constructively asking whether another approach could work better in a similar situation, for example. Such review done gently and lovingly serves to *coach* new greeters, not intended as criticism, but rather as encouragement to explore other possible ways the Holy Spirit may lead us to respond and proceed.

These post service meetings need to be short, but long enough to address your greeters' concerns. The benefit of these meetings, besides the excitement generated by sharing how the Holy Spirit has moved, is to minimize the need for many additional training sessions. It is on the job training and on the moment gratification!

Potential Training Topics for a Team meeting

What follows is a list of training topics. You may or may not want to cover them all, but rather use this list to spark your creativity.

Develop Empathy for Visitors

Empathy from personal experience goes a long way to solving and brainstorming ways to improve your church's greeting ministry. Invite your greeters to attend a worship service:

- Outside their tradition.
- By themselves.
- At a church they have never visited before.

For example, someone from a Pentecostal tradition could visit a Greek Orthodox Church, or an Episcopalian could visit a Vineyard. I attended an Evangelical Covenant church once when I did this exercise; another time I visited a Greek Orthodox Church where the service wasn't even conducted in English.

Encourage them to take a notebook and pen with them to write down their observations. Ask them to make notes of their experiences, specifically, what made them feel welcomed and/or uncomfortable. If your greeters do this in advance of your training session, plan to debrief these church visits in large or small groups.

The vision of hospitality ministry

Share your church's vision of a hospitality ministry. Stress the importance of greeting the people who come through your doors, whether they are members or regular attendees. Help greeters to see their part in the bigger picture of the hospitality ministry of our Lord Jesus.

Bible study on character

Consider developing a Bible study on the character of a greeter. You could use Galatians 5:22-25 on the fruit of the Holy Spirit. Challenge your greeters to think of practical ways to display those fruits while they are serving. How do they reflect the character of the Lord? Gently, suggest that we all need the Holy Spirit to grow and tend those qualities in our hearts, minds, thoughts and actions. Pray with them asking the Holy Spirit to fill them anew to mold their character more and more according to that of the Lord Jesus.

You could use the "one another" verses (see the next chapter). Or you could use Philippians 2:3-8 on servanthood. Consider Philippians 2:14-16 and think of ways you can "shine like stars." Have your greeters brainstorm ways this applies to the work, attitude, and character of a greeter.

Help Greeters with what to say

I speculate that some of the top queries that lead people to EvangelismCoach.org via Google seem to come from new greeters who are too embarrassed speak up when they are recruited. In the privacy of their own home, these new church greeters search the Internet for

- "How to say welcome to a church visitor"
- "Welcome Scripts for Church Guests"
- "Greetings to 1st time visitors at church"

- "A word of welcome for church visitors"
- "Welcome church visitors speech"
- "What to say to welcome visitors in a church"
- "How to say a welcome to visitors at church"
- "Tips on welcoming First timers in Church"

So, offer them suggestions. Perhaps you might want to consider giving a script to your new greeters.[2] Once people say something a few times, they might feel the liberty to relax and put their own flavor to it. Give your new greeters permission to explore approaches without fear of "messing up."

Let me share some possible beginning words of welcome which you can develop further into a resource for use at your church. Note that repeating the same line over and over may seem insincere.

- Welcome to [church name] this morning!
- God bless you.
- We're glad you are here this morning.
- Good morning and welcome to our church
- I've not met you yet! Welcome. My name is . . . .
- I don't believe I've met you yet. Have I?

Encourage your greeters to remain in a state of prayer that the Holy Spirit may grant fresh wisdom for how to address each new person or group of persons.

---

[2] Paige Lanier Chargois put an appendix in her book on greeters that gives some practical situational responses beyond opening statements. See The Work of the Greeter, pages 119-122.

How to recognize a visitor

One skill a greeter can learn is how to recognize a visitor. In your training, brainstorm some common characteristics of the body language of a first time visitor. Here are some examples:

- You don't recognize them.

- They appear tentative, hesitant.

- They seem unsure of where to go.

- They appear to be looking for signage.

- They stand alone or by themselves.

How to read body language

Body language can help determine the level of engagement that visitors and members want. For example, are their hands in their pockets? Is their pace slow or hurried? Are they distracted? Avoiding eye contact? You may want to include some tips on this particular area. Body language may suggest an underlying spiritual need that a careful greeter can learn.

> *I have my phone out at church so the greeters don't speak to me. — Twitter User*

How to explain the Gospel or offer prayer ministry

Sometimes, a person may feel the tug of the Holy Spirit in his or her heart. Maybe it is an awareness of God's sacred presence. Maybe it feels like the preacher is speaking directly to them. They might get up and walk out to the foyer to recompose themselves. An alert greeter may notice such people and feel prompted by the Holy Spirit to sit and talk with them for a while.

This happened to me during a conference. The speaker's topic spoke to the pain in my heart. I got up from where I sat and walked to the back of the auditorium so I wouldn't disturb the people around me. I couldn't leave – I wanted to hear more. I wanted to find the hope the preacher proclaimed. The pain inside of me expressed itself by quiet tears rolling down my cheeks. An observant usher noticed the interior struggle I was having. He approached me, and quietly asked me if I'd like to have him pray with me. We went to a back room off the sanctuary, where I experienced a very significant and healing time of prayer.

An astute greeter may be the right person at the right place to pray with someone for healing. The Holy Spirit may position a greeter at just the right time and place to help a visitor invite Christ to become Savior and Lord. Such a sacred privilege requires proper training. This doesn't happen all the time, but it would make for a great training topic to continue to grow up the ministry level of some of your more regular greeters.

Helping others to receive Jesus as Savior and Lord in prayer is the ultimate joy. Build into your training session adequate time and space to learn this art. In addition, make sure a greeter experienced in leading others to Christ is on hand each Sunday morning to whom less experienced greeters on duty may turn for help when the Holy Spirit moves.

Get Visitor Contact Information

If your greeters are in charge of getting first time visitor information, what is your process of training your greeters and ushers to get this information? What do they do with it once this information is obtained? I once gave a workshop to a group of hospitality leaders and no one knew what happened with this information once they turned it in. This was a case where division of labor had enforced such strict walls among groups of hospitality workers that the greeters never received the all important visitor contact information. And, they didn't even know what was done with it.

The actual mechanics of collecting visitor contact information are beyond the scope of this book. I interviewed an expert on the subject and recorded a radio interview to download as a free Mp3 in the podcast feed. See: http://www.evangelismcoach.org/2009/how-to-get-church-visitor-contact-information/.

Learn new names

Some churches encourage their greeters to learn at least one new name every week. This may seem unimportant, but I have found that people seem to appreciate it when you remember their name after a week. I noticed that the more names I remembered from week to week, the more likely it was for a visitor to return multiple times to our church, and eventually find a home with us. That is indeed anecdotal evidence. It may not be true with every visitor. But the dynamic of knowing and using another's name is clearly reflective of the character of our God who says, "Do not fear, for I have redeemed you; I have called you by name, you are mine" (Isaiah 43:1).

Brainstorm some ways you can help your greeters learn and remember a new name. Here are some examples:

- Review the visitor cards.
- Make a quick mental association.
- Use it in a genuine way in the conversation.
- Use a memory device (alliteration or image).

- Pray for the person by name during the week.

- Write it down on a little note card you keep in your pocket.

Encourage greeters to say goodbye to the new people they have met and to use their names. Intentionally saying goodbye goes the extra mile to show you care for them not only when they arrive, but when they leave as well. Your greeters might say "It was a pleasure to meet you this morning, Javier. I hope you will consider coming back to see us next week." Or "It was a pleasure to know you this morning, Ana. I hope to see you next week." Don't forget the children.

Decorum or Etiquette

If your church culture adheres to particular rules of decorum, make sure your greeters are acquainted with them and adhere to them. Some rules I've seen in churches:

- Men should wear a shirt, tie, slacks, and a suit coat. Women should wear a dress, pantsuit, blouse or skirt.

- The church does not permit food, drink, or gum inside the building.

- Do not seat people down the center aisle once the Procession has started.

- Do not reseat those who have left for a bathroom break during the reading of the Gospel.

- Keep the sanctuary doors closed once the service begins.

- A pair of ushers will be stationed half way to the front for escorting guests further into the sanctuary.

- Help parents remove noisy / crying babies.

You likely have some rules of decorum or etiquette that your greeters need to know. Don't assume they know them.

In the international church I served, we taught our greeters and members to introduce guests by name to the pastor who preached that week. That introduction is an honor in many cultures, so we made sure our greeters knew this as part of their training.

Common questions

Every greeter should know the general layout of your building, including where the water fountains and restrooms are located. That may seem like common sense, but remember, some of your new greeters may themselves be relatively new to your building and congregation.

If your greeters open the building and close it after the service, they should know the basics of the building layout, how to turn lights on and off, how to adjust heating/cooling, and how to handle the alarm systems.

A good practice may be to develop an FAQ list that can be distributed to new greeters. Update it with every rotation as you learn more common questions. Develop a list of basic questions that all your greeters can answer, such as

- Schedule of Services.
- The names of church leaders.
- Location of nursery, bathroom, and classrooms.
- Current announcements and church programming.
- Location of water fountains, first aid, telephones, and lost and found.

In your current context, what is the most common question that visitors ask? Ask your current greeters about the questions they are asked the most often to start generating this list. Add to it as you continue to recruit new greeters.

If you have a recent pictorial directory, give a copy to your new greeters and encourage them to get to know faces and names. If you display photos of new members on a wall, have your new greeters study those as well.

If your church uses hearing assistance devices or translation transmitters, greeters may need to know how to use the devices and system, as well as where they are stored and the processes for maintaining them. As part of their checklist, each one should know where extra batteries are.

Administrative Topics

I mention this briefly below. Many trainers find it effective for the new greeters to help develop, expand, and refine the list of policies. You might find it helpful to present a starter list for your group to brainstorm. Churches set various policies according to their own contexts. I raise these here to help you think through some of the policies you might want to cover.

How to handle schedule changes

Sometimes, life interrupts the best laid plans and schedules. As the ministry coordinator, think about what your procedure will be when a greeter can't make it because of a life emergency or last minute change. Are they responsible for finding a backup? Are they responsible for letting you know so that you can find a backup?

A good practice is to distribute a contact list of experienced greeters for current greeters to find their own backups. This relieves the administrative burden from you.

Lost and Found

Most churches have a section for lost and found. Bibles get left in the pews or chairs, cell phones fall out of pockets, and earrings fall to the floor. Settle on a protocol with your greeters to handle the loss of expensive items, in particular, so that their owners may find them quickly and safely.

Emergencies and Disturbances

Because of recent events involving church shootings, more congregations are evaluating security needs by thinking through the role greeters and ushers can play in emergency situations. Greeters are not expected to act like security guards, but since their assignment involves close observation of people and activity, they can be of great assistance during times of emergency, such as tornado, fire, or when someone faints or falls ill.

Since greeters are usually stationed around a facility in public areas and near the various entrances, it might be a good idea to discuss potential emergency situations in your training sessions.

As part of effective planning, prepare for when something happens, rather than react if it happens. Develop your own church's response to people who seem threatening, volatile, or to assess whether or not specific situations warrant a 911 call. What do your greeters need to know in such situations?

Communicating Needs that Greeters Discover

Greeters should be listening for needs as they interact with people. If some spiritual need comes up in a conversation with a greeter, what should that greeter do? Do they report it to the pastor? Pray with the individual on the spot?

Debriefing this on a regular basis with your greeters can help a church know what first time visitors are tending to need when they come through the doors. An attentive church leadership may use this information to help focus on and hone areas of ministry in the congregation.

Areas of assignment and scheduling

Choose areas where your greeters will serve or have greeters select where they want to serve. Some recruiters put people in particular places; others let volunteers select where they want to welcome people. One way is not better than the other, as long as you cover your bases.

Go over the schedule with your team. You may want to have your greeters pick the Sundays they can serve according to their schedules. Some may want to choose 3 months at a time. Others may choose one Sunday a month. Develop and post the schedule in a convenient place and as a ministry leader, keep one handy for your own reference.

Develop a checklist

Your volunteers want to do the right thing, and some might be nervous about making mistakes. Write up a simple ministry description of greeter instructions that can help put that person at ease. Write it specifically with your ministry context in mind. Checklists help memory and will help you meet the requirements your team has agreed upon.

The goal is not to overwhelm people with what they are to do. You're not writing a manual that covers all possible situations. Rather, set some expectations that are appropriate for your ministry context. For example, give some specific guidance concerning their time of arrival, how long to serve after the service starts, how to handle latecomers, and what clothing style is expected.

You may want to write out duties and expectations of the head greeter as distinct from the other greeters if the head greeter has more responsibilities.

Finally, a check list of tasks may help new greeters get oriented. Some churches post this small check list in a cabinet that contains supplies for greeters. I've included a sample check list in Appendix A.

Action steps – Chapter 5

1. Develop a list of frequently asked questions (FAQ) the answers to which all your greeters know well. Use some sort of FAQ that visitors commonly ask and have greeters know the answers. For example: where are the offices, telephones, bathroom, classrooms, exits, nursery, child care, events upcoming on the calendar.

2. Gather a list of new greeters. Set a training meeting date.

3. Plan an agenda for your first meeting. Take the sample agenda found in Appendix C, customize it for your own context, and hold your meeting.

4. Develop a duties or task check list. Develop a sample checklist that people can react to. Realize that they will modify, update, and change that list. If you have specialized teams (greeters, ushers, welcome center), develop lists for each one specific to their ministry area. See the sample I prepared in Appendix A.

Chapter 6.

The Character of a Greeter

The ministry of greeting is not something that can be done well by everyone. Some people are naturally gifted, some can learn a little more, but others ought to find another ministry. It takes certain skills and attitudes to serve as greeters. Personality and temperament go far in helping your members and guests feel welcome.

Since you are concerned as a greeting ministry leader to make the greeting experience one of the highest quality for the visitor to your church, ask the Lord for specific guidance in determining who are to serve as greeters and who are to render their service elsewhere in the ministry of the congregation.

Greeters are equipped for this ministry in the same way members of the Body of Christ are prepared for all aspects of Jesus' ministry: the Holy Spirit indwells us to conform us to Christ's character by growing His qualities in us, the fruit of the Holy Spirit (Galatians 5: 22-23).

Further, the Holy Spirit endows Christians with spiritual gifts, specific power to do Jesus' ministry far beyond our own natural abilities.

The following verse describes well a greeter's character and service:

> *Whatever you do, work at it with all your heart, as working for the Lord, not for people, since you know that you will receive an inheritance from the Lord as a reward. It is the Lord Christ you are serving. (Colossians 3:23-24)*

As greeter, keep in mind that they are serving the Body of Christ, and the individual "precious living stones" that make up the body, many of their duties will seem intuitive, and attitudes hopefully develop into ones that bear much fruit in the shaping of your church's greeting ministry.

Even if you have had a rotten morning—your hair wouldn't stay right, you spilled coffee on your pants in the car on your way to church, you were angered by a phone conversation during your commute—you are still called to serve the Body of Christ in kindness. Focus on the people coming in the door, not on yourself.

How do greeters express kindness at any given moment during the rush of Sunday morning service transitions?

A greeter is one who is able to quickly discern a person's immediate need and figure out a way to meet it with an attitude of kindness and joy, without any kind of expectation of a return.

Les Parrot has written an excellent chapter in his book <u>Serving as a Church Greeter</u>. His outline serves as the organizational basis for this chapter and is a good reminder to all of us about the importance of the "one another" commands in Scripture. He writes:

> *"Their much needed gifts and graces have been honed by adequate training and experience to raise their level of effectiveness, and the church foyer has been designated as their place of service. In warm-hearted churches everywhere, official church greeters have become the doers of a recognized ministry based on a biblical precedent"* (Parrot, 21).

Accept one another

Romans 15:7 read "Accept one another, then, just as Christ accepted you." Body language, not just words, conveys acceptance. A smile, a handshake, eye contact are all ways of focusing on another person and communicating acceptance. Instead of focusing on self, wondering how the other person is doing is a thought that goes a long way towards expressing acceptance.

Sometimes, this may mean taking undeserved heat. Frustrated parents, people who argued in the car on the way to church, someone who lost a friend to death the night before, may dump their anger or grief at the first happy greeter they encounter that morning. Some people arrive at church with an attitude, a chip on their shoulder and the greeter is the first person who bears the brunt of it.

This also speaks to people who are not like you. Many churches claim to honor diversity, but experience shows that some places are still not quite accepting of some kinds of diversity.

- Do you wonder if the Latino who just walked in is legal or not?

- Do you stare at the bar bell piercing through the right eye-brow?

- Do you visibly disapprove of the choice of clothing your guest made today?

Our body language communicates how we actually feel about others. Stares, gasps, and avoidance do not communicate acceptance. These body language movements are often reflexive. It requires a conscious, deliberate choice on our part to welcome those who are different from us. Practicing the unwavering smile of acceptance no matter who comes through your doors is not a bad idea. To greet the surprise visitor who is so *other* than the general demographic of your congregation, without negative body language, takes preparation and practice.

Honor one another

"Honor one another above yourselves" says the latter half of Romans 12:10. The New Living Translation goes onto say "Take delight in honoring one another."

Honor is a word that seems to have fallen out of use in Western Culture. In the Walker household, we've always taught the concept of honor to our kids. Actions are right and wrong based partly on whether or not the other party is honored. Tone of voice communicates honor or complaint. As we train up our children, we ask them to consider which actions bring the most honor to their sister or brother.

Honor places a high value on the other person. Holding a door open, making eye contact, helping another with a wet umbrella, all communicate honor to another. Escorting the lost visitor to a class, opening the sugar packet for the elderly woman with a hand tremor, and providing a translation device for the immigrant are all ways to show honor to your guests.

Another practical way of showing honor is asking about something you know is happening in the life of the person being greeted. "How is your mom doing?" "How did your test turn out?" "You have the results yet?" All of these questions demonstrate a level of honoring the other. People have often commented to me how much my little question meant. When people have called me when I miss a Sunday, I feel honored.

Be kind to one another

"Be devoted to one another in brotherly love" begins Romans 12:10. The Amplified version spells it out this way: "Love one another with brotherly affection as members of one family." The King James words it this way: "Be kindly affectioned one to another with brotherly love."

The act of greeting can demonstrate kindness in the midst of a world that is losing it. It is a world that is growing focused on speed, efficiency, process, and selfish arguments. Kindness sticks out and makes an impression. Helping the elderly who are losing muscle control in their hands to receive communion, taking a moment to listen to a person's grief, an appropriate human touch – all of these acts of kindness stick out in a cold and heartless world.

Parrot writes "the highest virtue among church greeters is their willingness to express human kindness. . . Suggest, lead, guide – or do anything else that is an extension of the human smile – but don't order people. Be a warm-hearted friend, not an officer" (33).

Learn to think "kindness."

Love one another

Romans 13:8 says "Love one another." The word choice indicates a type of love that is unconditional, and expressed in acceptance, honor, and kindness. Greeters display this kind of love through warm smile, a kind greeting, and an attitude that communicates a love of people.

It is a kind of love that greeters display in avoiding gossip or complaining, or bad-mouthing the church leadership. It is a love that speaks well of others, treats others well, and seeks to protect another's reputation. It is a love that is expressed without condition.

Not passing judgment on one another

Romans 14:13 reads "let us not pass judgment on one another any longer" (English Standard Version). Judgmental attitudes are displayed in body language: the cold shoulder, the stare at the funny hair color, the lack of eye contact and the disengagement that says "You are not welcome here." Judgmental attitudes are displayed in the choice of words to passively insult others, poke fun at people, and participate in gossip about the married parishioner caught in an affair over the weekend. The ministry of greeting is not the place for such judgment.

Greet one another

In Romans 16, Paul spends the first fifteen verses naming certain disciples of Christ he would like the church in Rome to greet. Then, he punctuates those requests with Romans 16:16, the most explicit passage on greeting in Romans: "Greet one another with a holy kiss." Paul repeats the command in 1 Corinthians 16:20 and 2 Corinthians 13:12.

Instead of a kiss, our North American culture encourages other ways of expressing human touch. For some, a warm hug is appropriate.

For others, it is a simple hand shake or a pat on the shoulder or back. I discuss this dynamic at length in the next chapter.

Action Steps – Chapter 6

1. Think of ways that you have experienced "one another" in greeting ministry, both as the assigned greeter and as the one being welcomed. Share how such ways of greeting have impacted you.

2. In what ways do these "one another" commands influence how you may choose to greet during your next opportunity?

3. Brainstorm practical ways you can connect these "one another" statements to your greeting ministry.

4. On a scale of 1-10, how do you rate yourself in these areas in the ministry of greeting? Where can you grow?

5. On a scale of 1-10, how would you rate your church in these areas in the ministry of greeting? Where can you grow?

6. What should a greeter say when someone speaks negatively to him/her about the pastor, the staff, the leadership, the worship service?

Chapter 7.

Duties of a Greeter

I'm sure it's wrong to use my position as a host team greeter at church to look at guys, but it just kinda happens (Twitter User).

Men and women of good character and the right spiritual gift mix have fun doing this ministry. Meeting new people, greeting familiar members, helping those who need assistance to get out of their car – all of it amounts to a joy filled ministry for people who love expressing their gifts in this greeting ministry. These volunteers tend to anticipate visitors' needs as if it is second nature, and then find ways to how to meet those needs quickly and easily.

But all volunteers do not know intuitively what to do when you call on them to serve as greeters. Thus, this chapter is geared to helping spell out some of the typical greeter duties.

Your church may have designed ministries in addition to the greeting ministry that are responsible for some of the assignments. For example, a crew can be established with the sole purpose of opening the church and seeing that it is locked up and secure at the end of the morning. This frees the greeters to focus exclusively on people. In

North America, most congregations worship fewer than 100 people on Sunday morning. In these congregations, it probably makes sense for the greeters to prepare the building as well.

Watch your own bias. If you are the recruiter or head of the greeting ministry, be conscious of your own perspective and personality. It may seem to be common sense to you ("Of course I walk up to strangers and greet them") but it may not be common sense to some of your volunteers.

Most of the recruiters with whom I have spoken lean toward the extrovert / outgoing type of personality. If that is you as well, keep in mind that what is safe, comfortable, and intuitive to you, may not be to some of your volunteers who need more explicit guidance.

What does a greeter do?

These are general guidelines, meant to spur your thinking. Adjust for your needs, and continue to adapt as your greeting ministry grows and matures.

The basic skills required are a love for the Lord Jesus and your congregation, the ability to smile warmly and genuinely, and a sharp eye to detect a need and know how to meet it. If you choose to use volunteers who are not yet believers, they should have a genuine respect for Jesus as they continue to their journey towards faith.

If you are just starting a greeting ministry for your church, realize you can't prescribe responses for every possible situation greeters may encounter. Start and remain with the basic principles. If your greeters know them well, the Holy Spirit will help them act on the principles in the moment and with a flourish of their own personalities to find an appropriate application to meet the given need.

Both as recruiter and as greeter, use common sense. Think of the principles.

- "Show hospitality one to another."
- "Greet one another."
- "Love one another as Christ loved the church."

Your debriefing meeting after worship becomes the ideal setting for reviewing how the Holy Spirit enabled us to welcome others, where we managed well to meet needs, and what we can learn for the next time. With the founding principles in mind and heart, we learn by doing, watching, listening, and accepting constructive direction for improvement. The greeting ministry is to be fun expression of showing love to the people the Holy Spirit brings to you on Sunday.

Spiritual Preparation

Encourage your greeters to take some time and pray before the service, whether or not you hold an all greeting crew meeting prior to the service. Pray about the role that you will fulfill that day. Pray about the people that you will meet. Ask the Lord to give you insight into the people that you will meet and that you will have ability to minister to their needs.

Physical Preparation

Fresh breath. It can go without saying, but it still needs to be said—however you get that fresh breath, sprays, gum, mouthwash, strips, use it. As one of my website commentators emailed me,

> *"You don't want the Word of Life to be hindered by the Breath of Death."*

This can be particularly true as many people bring their morning coffee with them. Brush your teeth before you come and carry a mint or something to crush the coffee breath.

Deodorant. You can likely think of times when you wish you had put some on, or that the person you were hugging had some.

Colognes / Perfumes. Some people have instant reaction to strong odors, good or bad. Be careful with perfumes and colognes. Mild use may be ok, but too much is not a good thing. Personally, strong cologne causes an overactive histamine reaction in me – instant watery eyes, and the phlegm begins to form. Sometimes I cough uncontrollably. Consider what you think is appropriate. Do I still smell you after you've left the room? That's likely too much.

Appropriate attire. Your particular church determines this. Some churches require their greeters to wear uniforms. Some expect coats and ties for the men and dresses for the women. Others are okay with business casual. Choose what is appropriate for your church culture. In one church I attended, the greeters bought and paid for the uniforms the church selected for them—a privilege of serving in that ministry. It was clear to me, a visitor, that they were staff of some kind and could likely answer my questions.

Don't be too informal, as visitors tend to form their first impression of your church from how you are dressed. Dress neatly in what is appropriate for your church. If people dress up for church, do the same. If it's business casual, go similarly.

General Duties

Wash hands before and after. As more and more people are health conscious, even germ-phobic, wash your hands regularly throughout the morning. Or, better, stock up on those little gel hand sanitizers—they are a modern marvel. With our current awareness of germs, be careful with young infants.

> *Sneezing in the hand is nasty. I avoid shaking the greeter's hand @ church because he shakes 2-500+ hands before mine! (Twitter User)*

Give margin. We've all been guilty of waking up too late, rushing though our morning, scarfing down a pre-cooked breakfast item from the freezer or grabbing a pastry from the local coffee shop, and speeding in the car to get to church on time. We arrive stressed, perhaps irritated, and maybe a little disheveled in our appearance. One time, I rushed to church in this way only to discover during the communion prayer that I had on two different-colored brown shoes. Both brown, but clearly not a pair!

On the mornings you are slated to greet, give yourself plenty of margin. Take the time to eat correctly, have your devotional time, and reflect on the calling you are about to fulfill that morning. Go to bed early the night before.

Arrive early. Greeters should arrive 15-20 minutes prior to the service. This gives them time to do what they are expected to prepare themselves and their areas for the work of the ministry. If they are responsible for opening up the building, they may need more time.

Some visitors arrive early, some will arrive just in time, and others will be late. Be available to cover all those bases. If a parent arrives late with a small child, an attentive and available greeter can calm as stress and harried parent with a kind word and a helpful hand.

Prepare or Tidy up your areas. Some churches will have their greeters responsible for opening the building, setting thermostats, turning on the lights, and preparing the hearing assistance devices. Make sure the doors are unlocked and open.

Other greeters might be responsible for a tidy up of their area and rapidly removing the junked bulletins between services. A quick notice of litter, trash, discarded bulletins and out of date announcement fliers serves as ideas to help tidy up an area.

Locate bulletins or programs. Take a quick read to be familiar with the events and announcements. Locate your information packets if you use them.

Wear your name badge. Many churches will give their greeters some kind of badge that identifies them as official staff for the service. If your church provides you with a badge or name tag, wear it proudly as a member of the team. In other places, a uniform might accomplish this same goal. Be sure you know where nametags or lanyards are stored and put them back after the service is over.

Presence. Serve in your role with dignity. You are a representative of the church you serve. Slouching against the wall is a big no-no. Stand properly, but relaxed. Find what is normal and acceptable in your church for serving and stay within those boundaries. The purpose of this ministry is not to make a statement about the world or your inner emotional attitude, but to serve those who walk in the door.

Make Eye Contact. As you greet, be sure to make friendly eye contact with people. In April of 2009, Dominoes pizza had a public relations problem with an employee video posted on You Tube. The CEO went on camera to offer an apology and to speak about what the

Chris Walker

company was doing to address the situation. Not once, did he look into the camera at his audience. He appeared to be reading something scripted, off to the side of the camera.

It has been observed by some that President Obama is a great orator when he has a teleprompter, but since he doesn't often look into the TV camera, we don't feel any sense of connection with him.

Smile. Don't fake it. Let your smile be genuine. According to Paul Ekman, who developed the fake smile test[3] and whose researched determined there are 43 muscles that create 10,000 visible facial configurations, of which 3,000 are meaningful[4], a smile has a welcoming ability. "We can pick up a smile from 30 meters away. A smile lets us know that we are going to get a positive reception and it's hard not to reciprocate."[5]

Take the smile test (if remains online) and see what score you get. When I took the smile test, I picked up 100% of the fake smiles of the 20 that were presented. For example, smiling without eye contact is perceived as false. Offer eye contact and a sincere smile and you'll make a great first impression.

Body language. Strike an open posture. Some coach their greeters to think about making sure you point your heart to the heart of the person you are greeting, that is, heart to heart. Fully face the person you are greeting and make sure you have their attention, and that they have yours.

---

[3] Found at http://www.bbc.co.uk/science/humanbody/mind/surveys/smiles/ (Accessed October 2009)
[4] http://www.sfgate.com/cgi-bin/article.cgi?f=/c/a/2002/09/16/MN241376.DTL&type=science (Accessed October 2009)
[5] Quoted in Fusion: Turning First-Time Guests into Fully-Engaged Members of Your Church, Nelson Searcy, p. 56.

107

Be attentive. As you greet people, whether members or visitors, think about the needs they may have. Part of excelling in the art of greeting is being able to assess a possible need and provide a solution for it quickly.

Watch for practical needs. Let me give a couple of possible situations. What would you do as a greeter to meet a perceived need?

- A visitor walks in from the rain with a wet umbrella.

- It's cold. Everyone comes wearing heavy jackets.

- A single dad walks in with his 2 year old daughter.

- A car drives up to the main entrance to drop off an elderly woman with a walker.

- A man makes his way past several people without saying hello to anyone and walks straight to the sanctuary.

Beyond practical ways to serve, watch for deeper needs. Be ready to speak with visitors and members who seem to be hurting, visibly sad or distracted. Ask the Father for the Holy Spirit's guidance. Your quiet presence may allow your visitor to share the concern with you briefly. Depending on the nature of this personal need, you and one of your team may step aside with this person for private prayer. You may decide to meet again another day over coffee so that you can continue to be a friend with a listening ear. And, or, you may discern that your pastor is needed. If this person would like to meet with your pastor, follow your congregation's practice of how to bring the two together after worship to make an appointment.

Greet Everyone. Many times, greeters and ushers are the first impression others have of our churches. You want your greeters to meet everyone with a smile, making him or her feel welcome.

It's easy to focus on just the people you know. We all know it is easier to greet friends than it is to greet strangers. Let us keep our focus. I strongly encourage you to learn to enjoy the discovery of new names and potential new friends. Your service as greeter is to be the initiator of friendliness.

You should also greet the children as they walk in. I've collected a few stories of children who remember the greeter because the greeter took the time to say hello. I'm also familiar with people who chose their church because a greeter made the effort to say hello to their children.

Depending on the pace of people entering, you might have the time to inquire, "How is the family?" or "How are you doing?"

Extend a hand. In North America, a hand shake is a common greeting practice. As you greet people, extend your open hand to receive the hand of your guest. Most will accept it, some will not. Let your visitor or fellow church member guide you into how they would like to be greeted.

Do not grip too tightly, as some people may have had painful arthritis or elbow surgery the week before. Be gentle, but firm. No need for floor to ceiling pumping action, and no need for a limp wristed approach either. Remember: two or three small up and down pumps, then let go!

A handshake was a practice frowned upon in the 1920s, but is a common practice today. It is one culturally appropriate way to replace "greet one another with a holy kiss" (1 Corinthians 16.20; 2 Corinthians 13:12). Human touch needs to be culturally appropriate and healthy.

I am often asked about hugs. A friendly hug is a warm way of expressing affection. Yet, I don't think hugs are appropriate when greeting first time visitors. Sure, you can do that with people you know well, but in our North American environment, it is not likely a good practice towards first time visitors. I feel awkward when someone I don't know defends their initiative to hug me with a dismissive "I'm a hugger" and proceeds to hug me. Don't put your visitor in this uncomfortable situation.

I work in Hispanic cultures where women greet each other the second time they meet with a cheek to cheek air kiss. In some Latin American countries I have visited, the hand shake is not hand to hand, but a wrist grab. At first, I thought I was missing a person's hand, but learned that in that context, it was a sign of intimate welcome, friendlier than a business style hand to hand greeting we are used to in the United States.

Determine the appropriate way to initiate a greeting in your culture and use it.

Engage people in conversation. Not every position in the greeting ministry allows for extended conversations. People file into the church rapidly in the minutes before the service starts. After worship, most everyone exits quickly. All to say, there is often little time for a conversation at the greeting line by the entry door.

But if you get the chance to talk with people, don't just be limited to ritual kindness "How are you?" "I'm fine" or discussing the weather or last night's sports game. Ask people about their lives, themselves. Other-oriented conversation communicates genuine care. You might learn of a need that needs pastoral follow-up. Feel free to pass that along to ministry leaders or your pastor.

When you are talking with people you know, keep the first time visitor in mind. You can very easily excuse yourself from a conversation with a friend to make an initial contact with someone you don't know or just have met.

Listen. One of your primary tasks is to listen to people and respond to some of their needs when possible. You might be asked for directions to the bathrooms or the nursery, as two examples. People may also feel free to express their spiritual needs with you. Listen carefully to hear their questions clearly. Be careful not to overwhelm people with too much information. Informational questions can be answered simply. If you are attempting to greet many people all at once, it is perfectly acceptable to point information seekers to the Welcome Center.

Notice the Visitor. Notice the unknown guest. Extend a welcome. Take the initiative, and greet the stranger. Be on the lookout for people you don't recognize. Take the risk of talking with the stranger. The experience of hospitality begins with such initiative.

Some people are shy. Preserve their dignity by not being too forward. Others are gregarious and want to be asked questions. Attempt to discern one from another. Be as helpful as you can.

People come to church burdened with hurts, disappointments and personal crises. As you have opportunity, steer hurting people to those in the church family who can best help—the pastor, professional or peer counselors, teachers, physicians, social workers. Use your knowledge to meet people at their points of need.

Make appropriate small talk. One question I've learned not to ask people is whether they're "new here" or "Is this your first time here?" If they answer no, the next moment is sure to be awkward however they handle it. If they answer yes, they are new, they may feel even more like the outsiders they are.

Instead, when you don't recognize people, simply welcome them to your church, introduce yourself, and say that you don't think you've met them before. Here are some possible things I have found helpful to say.

- Welcome to [church name] this morning!
- God bless you.
- We're glad you are here this morning.
- I've not met you yet! Welcome.

Make sure you are not using the same phrase over and over again. It sounds insincere. Put your own personality into it and vary your statements, even slightly, for freshness.

Introduce the Visitor. Some places make it a practice for the greeter to introduce the visitor BY NAME to another friend in the church. I recently heard a story of a gentleman who visited a church across the street from the one he wanted to attend. A greeter introduced himself, learned his name, and then introduced him personally by name to 5 or 6 other people that morning. The gentleman telling the story remembers this greeter's name, but nothing else about the church. This greeting stood out in his mind.

Take people where they need to go. Some visitors need directions to find a rest room, the children's classes, or the nursery. Instead of saying "take the first left, go up the stairs, and hang a right and go to the family life center," simply take the person. If you don't have the liberty to leave your spot, grab a friend who can take them.

This helps remove the anxiety of getting lost. I've noticed that when I can't find something in one of those big box stores, and someone says, "Let me take you," I find myself more at peace than having to remember "somewhere in the middle of isle 8 in the green zone across from the employee restrooms."

If you can only give directions, don't use churchy language. Your visitor might not know what narthex is, where to find a chancel, or which closet belongs to the sexton. They certainly don't know which room was the Millard room, or where the Garrison class meets. Use everyday language.

Connect visitors. In your conversations, you might encounter ways to connect other people to your new friend. I remember a pastor who would do this by saying, for example, "I need to introduce you to John who works in your field." Then, he would nod to the greeter who would escort the visitor to John. "John," the greeter would say, "I'd like to introduce you to Peter. He's researching drug receptors just like you are for your PhD. He's visiting our church for the first time today." As a greeter, look for connections among your friends in the church who have things in common.

Think of the Visitor Every Sunday. Although you rotate off formal greeting duty on certain Sundays, remain on the lookout for the visitor. From my own experience it can be more profound and impressive for the visitor to be greeted by someone who is "not the professional with the nametag" and doesn't have to do it.

Use Common Sense. A few written policies and basic checklists are helpful. Some may try to go beyond helpful policies and try to put in a list of everything that greeters are not supposed to do. You don't need to develop an exhaustive list of what not to do. I found the following list of 14 prohibitions in a church whose name I will not disclose:

- Don't slouch against the wall.

- Don't enter the bathroom with them.

- Don't enter into extended conversations.

- Don't evaluate the visitor for social status.

- Don't ask 20 questions or conduct a doctrinal exam.

- Don't give a crushing handshake with wild arm pumping action.

- Don't prescreen visitors before letting them into the sanctuary.

- Don't serve if you have a head cold, an open wound, or skin condition.

- Don't use heavily scented hand lotion the day you are greeting.

- Don't forget to bathe.

- Don't forget to brush your teeth.

- Make sure to brush the dandruff off your clothes.

- Don't dress inappropriately.

- Don't talk or socialize with other greeters or members while visitors pass you by.

- Don't use teenagers since they don't have the assertiveness to take initiative and adults are not expected to be greeted by teens. (my note: Ouch!)

As the recruiter or as a greeter, use common sense. Think of the principles: "Show hospitality one to another," "Greet one another," "Love one another as Christ loved the church." A lot of these prohibitions will be intuitive when the principles are kept in mind. Greeting ministry is to be fun. Making a huge list of do's and don'ts cuts down on the fun.

Find your own replacement. Life happens and your plans may have to change. Ask the greeting ministry coordinator for a contact list of experienced greeters and find your own substitute. This helps relieve the burden on the greeting ministry coordinator from having to deal with this last minute need. The coordinator should be the backup person of last resort. You might want to inform your coordinator that you've found a substitute, and who she or he is.

Assist people with disabilities. This likely deserves a whole book itself. As the baby boomers get older, as more veterans return home injured from the wars in Iraq and Afghanistan, and as people are involved in accidents of all kinds, you will likely encounter people with some kind of disability.

Work with your recruiter or trainer—your parish nurse, if you have one, for special training in order to offer the most helpful assistance possible. Your church might want to consider mobility devices for use on Sunday, if one has been forgotten. Some churches keep a wheelchair and walker on site for just this kind of emergency. Greeters should know where these items are kept and help people use them and return them.

When the service is over

Focus groups have indicated that the most common time for visitors to reflect on and evaluate the friendliness of a congregation is right after the service is over. This is an opportunity for your greeters to go the extra mile once again to look for the first time visitors they greeted on the way in, to smile and say, "Glad you were here today." Further, this is the ideal time to introduce them to church members at hand.

Be intentional about inviting them to the post service reception, the coffee hour. This is a good time to engage them in further conversation about themselves, the worship service, and what they are looking for in a home church.

Offer to pray with visitors if it seems appropriate.

This could also be a good time to make a note of new visitors that you met. Use that list as a mental reminder the next week so that you can greet them by name if they have returned.

You might also want to re-tidy your area in preparation for the greeting team next week. Give a rapid walk through the sanctuary to pick up stray bulletins, return Bibles to the rack, put your supplies or nametags away, and do things that you think will honor the team serving in this role the next week.

Finally, take a moment to pray, thanking God for the people you met today.

A word about ushers

The role of usher is to assist and aid the Pastor, staff, and congregation during the worship service as needed. Most of their area of focus is within the sanctuary. Sometimes they are also involved in preparing the sanctuary for the service, such as lighting candles or removing the cloth covering from organ or piano, for examples.

They are the ones who likely pass out bulletins. Ushers should read the bulletin first thing upon their arrival. It is an unfortunate and unnecessary occurrence, if, for example, the bulletin says, "reports are at the back of the church" or, makes reference to the "enclosed insert," when the reports are *not* available at the back of the church, and there is no enclosed insert. It's called preparation. Lack of preparation and attention to details do not speak well of your congregation.

In churches without air-conditioning, the ushers are probably the ones to pass out fans.

Ushers guide people to their seats, answer last minute questions, all with a smile. Here is where all this greeter information comes in handy. Ushers are usually the last link in the official process of greeting, the important infrastructure which supports and encourages your church members not on greeter duty to become themselves more open and welcoming of your visitors.

In more liturgical churches, an usher can perhaps ask a visitor, "Would you like to sit with a member who can help you follow the worship service?" I've talked with several friends who were appreciative of a seat mate helping them know when to kneel, when to stand, and find the song in the prayer book or hymnal.

If your church has large-print bulletins, Bibles and hymnals on hand, your ushers may offer them to those with vision difficulties. Since that assumption could prove awkward, an usher could ask simply, "How can I help you participate this morning?"

Ushers seat latecomers according to a congregation's protocol, whether at specific times only, in order to limit the way worship is disturbed, or whenever and however they may slip in. Some congregations do not seat latecomers under any circumstances during the reading of the Scriptures, or during the pastoral prayer or the offering. Develop your working guidelines as to when and how to seat latecomers.

Ushers collect the offering. The formality of how the offering is collected is often determined by the tradition of your church. Is it an orderly procession of passing the plates, or is a joyous march forward to a common receptacle that the ushers pick up afterwards? Or is it so informal the pastor asks every week, "Can I have a few ushers to take up the offering?"

As part of their duties, ushers should know where the offering collecting devices are stored (plates, baskets, pouches, or box). Of course, they need to know how the collection is taken up according to your church's custom. Finally, they need to know the process of turning in the collection to those who count the offering.

Some ushers are also given the responsibility of counting heads during the service. If your church tracks the numbers of worship attendees, this is a great place to get it done.

In some church contexts, ushers also assist any ministry in response to altar calls. When pastors give the invitation to come to the front, the ushers also step forward to help guide the respondents.

In more charismatic traditions, the ushers curb worshippers' enthusiasm from getting out of control. They may set boundaries clearly so that worshippers know exactly *where* they may dance before the Lord, if they wish to. Ushers may help those who need intensive prayer to the prayer room where the prayer team is waiting. If resting in the Spirit is a practice in your congregation, ushers may also be catchers. They can provide blankets for women.

Ushers may also be responsible for clean-up after worship: removing discarded bulletins, collecting pew register pads, putting Bibles and hymnals back in their places.

Action steps – Chapter 7:

1. What are the qualities of a greeter that you want to nurture and grow?

2. What are your greeters responsible for?

3. Develop a checklist of greeter / usher responsibilities and have it posted where they can make quick reference before and during the service.

Appendix A
Sample Greeter Checklist

Here is a sample checklist. Develop your own and post it in various discreet areas for quick reference for your volunteers.

- Arrive 20 minutes before service

- Find you name tag and put it on.

- Locate connection cards and make sure you use them.

- Spot check foyer/lobby for cleanliness and tidiness.

- Solve logistical problems as needed (are bulletin inserts available, sign up lists where they are said to be).

- Confirm that hearing assistance devices and extra batteries are ready.

- Confirm the availability of the church newsletter

- Are Children's goody bags ready for distribution?

- Make sure appropriate candles are lit.

- Continue serving for 20 minutes after the service to seat latecomers.

- Offer to put wet umbrellas in umbrella bags. Make sure they are ready.

- After the service, seek out first time visitors. Invite them to the coffee break.

- Lock up the doors, turn out the lights and turn off ceiling fans.

Appendix B.
Brainstorming Procedural Questions

Because there are so many church contexts and cultures, you need to develop your own list. Feel free to add and subtract.

1. How does your church handle late arrivals? What role shall greeters play in helping those who arrive late?

2. How will your greeting team handle emergencies and disruptions?

3. What is your visitor contact information process? Are greeters/ushers expected to collect that information?

4. Are greeters responsible for the visitor packets at the information table? Likewise, are they sure the table is adequately stocked?

5. Who maintains your church's decorum? That is, who monitors the foyer after the service has begun? Who is on hand with the authority to discourage gum chewing, for example, in worship? Who assists parents with crying children during worship?

6. Where do greeters station themselves?

7. How many layers of greeting do you want?

8. Is it reasonable to challenge your greeters to learn a new name each week?

9. What do you want greeters to say?

10. Do you want your regular greeters to know CPR?

11. Who is responsible for open up (unlocking the doors) and closing up (locking them back up and setting the alarm)?

12. Are your greeters for the first service in charge of turning on the lights and making sure the bathrooms are stocked with paper products?

13. Umbrellas – what do you with wet ones?[6]

14. Where is the Lost and Found? What happens if a greeter finds an expensive piece of jewelry or cell phone?

15. What is your greeter's response when a person seeks financial or food assistance during the service?

16. What is your administrative response to prayer concerns or needs that are shared with your greeters?

17. How do you follow up with those who want to become members or make a profession of faith in Christ as Savior and Lord?

18. Who is responsible for preparing the sanctuary for worship? The ushers, the deacons, the greeters, or nobody?

19. Who lights the candles?

20. Who makes sure the visitor cards are well stocked and in the right place?

21. Who oversees the hearing assistance devices? Fresh batteries available?

22. Who makes sure last week's bulletin is not stuffed in the pew rack?

---

[6] See http://www.brenmarco.com/category/pos/wet_umbrella_bags. They have eco-friendly designs as well. I've not used them, just giving you an idea, not a recommendation. Pick your own vendor.

23. Who is responsible for straightening the cards in the foyer, pencils, and attendance pads?

24. Who is responsible for the goodie bags for children or thank you for visiting gifts for first time visitors?

25. What positive traits do you want your visitors to see in your greeters?

Appendix C.
Sample Greeter Training Workshop

I include here a sample workshop structure that may work in your context. You may want to provide lunch. It is an unspoken rule in the seminar business — better turn out when you provide good food. A light meal, catered lunch, or something edible increases your turnout.

You can use the meal time for informal conversations related to the topic at hand. For example: Have the table leader people to share stories where they felt really welcome – a conference, cruise, hotel, or meeting. Allow enough time for everyone to share at least one story. Ask how it felt to be welcomed? What did the hosts do to help create those feelings?

What follows below is a sample agenda with some of the major parts of a suggested meeting. Exercises are included.

Plan on 2-3 hours, maybe more depending on how much you want to accomplish. If you are launching a new greeter ministry, consider initially taking up to 6 hours to help design the ministry. Two other good workshops training schedules can be found in

- Paige Lanier Chargois, The Work of the Greeter. (Appendix)

- Mark Waltz, First Impressions Ministry: Creating Wow Experiences in Your Church. (Chapter 8 with exercises scattered throughout).

The vision of your church's hospitality.

Summarize your church's vision for hospitality, the overall big picture of ministry values, and the goal to help members and guests feel welcome. This may be a good place to have the senior pastor share the vision, and maybe a great place to have your church's governing board attend.

Share biblical study of the alien from Leviticus. See http://www.evangelismcoach.org/2008/you-were-a-church-visitor/

Share your experiences of visiting other churches to cast vision as to why this is personally important to you.

If your church has confused evangelism with hospitality, this may be a good place to draw the distinction between them. [7] Essentially, hospitality focuses on the first time visitor experience, while evangelism focuses on the proclamation and hearing of the gospel. The former looks for a return visit, while the second looks for a changed life.

Discuss and share hospitality stories from the Bible.

Personal Visit Stories.

If your greeters took the challenge of visiting other churches before they came to the training meeting, have them share their first hand experiences. Empathy with the first time visitor will give your group tremendous insight. When one remembers what it feels like not to feel welcomed, one is more likely to be welcoming.

---

[7] I develop this distinction further in Chapter 3 of my other ebook, How to Welcome Church Visitors, available only at http://www.welcomechurchvisitors.com/.

Stories from current visitors.

Do the "who is your visitor" exercise. If you collect contact information, or any type of post visit survey, share the stories. For example, review some names and faces from the last few weeks. What do you know and remember about your visitors? Who is your typical visitor? What is the general demographic makeup of your visitors? What are common needs of your visitors? Some churches ask for feedback from their visitors. Retain this information for your next training meeting.

Guidelines for duties and expectations.

Review your current checklist and duties list with your greeters. Brainstorm any changes or additions. Consider telling stories as to why some of those items are in the checklist if some of them are recent additions.

Role Play

Develop some ministry role plays. I've offered you a few in Appendix D. Put a situation up on the screen or flip chart. Have your table groups pick a person to be the greeter, one to be a visitor, and the rest observers. Allow each person in the group to share observations and thoughts about the role play, players and observers alike.

Appendix D.
Sample Training Exercises

First Impressions.[8]

Imagine a social or business setting into which you walk. What is your first thought? Take a moment to make a note of your first thought – Don't think hard, just write down your first thoughts that come to mind:

- Starbucks

- Your last hotel stay

- Your last visit to a big-box store like Home Depot or Wal-Mart

- Your most recent visit to a boutique or specialty shop

- Your bank

Allow time for team members to talk about where they shop, the products or stores to which they are loyal. Goal: understand the consumer that walks into your church.

---

[7] Exercise inspired from Mark Waltz, First Impressions Ministry: Creating Wow Experiences in Your Church. (19)

Brainstorm what Awesome Hospitality Looks Like.[9]

Decide how you want your visitors to describe their experience with you. Have each team member write down his or her top three words.

Tally them up. Vote on the three most popular ones.

Print them on posters, wallet cards and inner-office materials.

This will keep your hospitality philosophy in front of people's faces, thus holding them *Accountable* to and giving them *Ownership* of a decision to which they contributed. What is your service philosophy?

Tell your own story.

Hold a small group discussion where members share personal stories of why they connected and remain connected to your church.

Goal: To recognize the theme of personal relationships as paramount expressed by hospitality.

Body Language First impressions

Observe the people around your table.

I notice _____

I see _____

I think / imagine _____

Discuss what you notice with the people you observe and see if you are accurate.

Goal: to become aware of initial thoughts and judgments about people based on the physical observation of them.

---

[9] Inspired by one of my favorite blogs:
http://hellomynameisscott.blogspot.com/2009/10/you-dont-have-to-be-ritz-carlton-to.html
(Accessed October 5, 2009)

Take the smile test.

If you have a live internet connection with a high speed connection, project or display the smile test (http://www.bbc.co.uk/science/humanbody/mind/surveys/smiles/) up on the wall and have your people guess. Distribute to your participants a worksheet numbered 1-20, with Fake and Genuine Columns.

As the organizer, take it yourself ahead of time so that you are familiar with it.

Discuss the results and the importance of a smile in your greeting ministry.

Be the visitor.

At least once during the 4 weeks prior to the training event, make a personal and solo visit to a church outside your denominational tradition.

For example, if you are a Presbyterian, pick a local Pentecostal congregation. If you are a Baptist, pick an Episcopal church. (Remove the comfort of the familiar).

Pick one of a similar size to yours to help you make a legitimate comparison.

Do not knowingly pick a friend's church. Pick a church that you have never visited, and attend by yourself (remove all the comfort of having a friend with you).

Goal: Empathize with the first time visitor experience.

Who is our Visitor?[10]

Pick a couple of recent visitor contact cards. Choose a couple of anonymous prayer requests, if you collect them. Make photo copies ahead of time and distribute to the table groups.

Have each group of people determine what they can about your typical visitor. Develop a guest profile based on intuitive assumptions from the very limited information on the contact cards and prayer requests. What do they like? What are their needs? Where do you think they shop? Who are their friends? Are they married, single, divorced, widowed? Are they in school? What might they study? What are their goals / dreams? Why did they come to church?

Ask for a show of hands among your group if they have had similar prayer requests to those mentioned on the card. The goal is self-identification. The gap between your greeter and visitor just got a little smaller. Take some time as a group to pray for the needs on the prayer cards before moving on to the next part of your training session.

Brainstorming Exercises.

Brainstorm "10 tips for new greeters."

Brainstorm "10 painful mistakes to avoid."

Brainstorm "10 obstacles to a comfortable visit to your church."

Compile this list. Add to it or subtract from it each time you conduct a training event.

---

[10] Inspired by First Impressions: Creating Wow Experiences In Your Church, Mark Waltz (p. 91). Pages 93-96 offer some more training exercises that would be useful.

Role play some possible scenarios.

Have fun with this exercise. Allow time for each group to role play and have members discuss their observation as the greeter, as the guest, and as an observer. Let these be self-guided discussions.

- You observe an elderly woman who has weak motor controls in the hand. How will you assist her to receive communion out of those little cups before she spills it on herself?

- Father with a toddler in tow and a baby in his arms.

- Pregnant teenage girl, oversized shirt, overgrown bangs, and brow piercings.

For Further Reading

This list refers to some of the books I have used to help me develop this material along with all the conversations I've had with many people via ChurchGreeterTraining.com. You should be able to click on the titles to order your copies from Amazon (affiliate links).

Les Parrot, Serving as a Church Greeter. Slightly outdated, but good theological and historical overview. One chapter goes off topic into first impressions area like cleaning the church, and checking your signage. Useful for a greeting recruiter or trainer.

Annette Schroeder, Welcome to Our Church: Very outdated and has conflicting advice. Uses rare vocabulary. Recommends some practices that have proven not to be effective. Can serve as a research tool, but not a team book.

Paige Lanier Chargois, The Work of the Greeter. Published in 2009, this work is the most recent one I've found that doesn't feel out of date. A much needed improvement over existing Greeter books.

Buddy Bell, Ushering 101 and Greeting 101. The stories suggest the general audience to be more of the Pentecostal / Charismatic tradition where a traditional high respect for the pastor is normative. Some practical tips and advice. But some of his stories might be a worldview stretch for some in the more mainline faith traditions.

Gary McIntosh, <u>Beyond the First Visit: The Complete Guide to Connecting Guests to Your Church</u>. Title suggests book focuses on assimilation, but it is concentrated on hospitality, marketing, and preparing your worship space.

Mark Waltz, <u>First Impressions Ministry: Creating Wow Experiences in Your Church</u>. Great recent text on hospitality and impressions with lots of useful principles. Most of the examples are geared towards larger churches with multiple services, multiple campuses. Small churches can find helpful ideas in the midst of the stories.

Nelson Searcy, <u>Fusion: Turning First-Time Guests into Fully-Engaged Members of Your Church</u>. Focused more on assimilation processes than on actual greeting.

About EvangelismCoach.org

EvangelismCoach.org is a website resource on evangelism training and practical church growth. Launched in 2007, it has evolved into an international evangelism training ministry focused on helping churches in the Americas (from Alaska to Chile) re-discover a passion for evangelism and growing the Church in the power of the Holy Spirit.

I want to help you increase the number of conversations that lead people towards Christ. We come along side churches, mission organizations, and individuals to provide specialized evangelism training, mentoring, and coaching in effective evangelism and church growth.

Chris has studied evangelism and church growth ever since answering phones for a Billy Graham crusade over 20 years ago, and has led countless training seminars throughout North and South America in many different denominations.

If you want to receive new articles as soon as they are released at the website, be sure to grab the Friday email that I offer at the website. Visit http://www.EvangelismCoach.org and find the Friday update at the top of the site or under the comment box of any article.

More Evangelism Coach Hospitality Resources:

Visit http://www.EvangelismCoach.org/store to see additional hospitality resources by EvangelismCoach.org. You can find resources for hospitality committees and welcome ministry leaders who want to start looking at their hospitality systems, but are not sure where to start.

- Audio Download on How to Do a Church Hospitality Review
- Audio Download on Casting the Vision for Hospitality – Creating that Culture
- Ebook – How to Welcome Church Visitors
- Greeter Training DVDs 1 and 2 (Recorded Webinars)
- Break the Unseen Barriers DVD set (3 DVDs). Free introduction videos at http://www.ChurchHospitalityTraining.com

You can receive ongoing coaching in church hospitality, a private webinar training for your team, or a weekend conference for your church. Contact Chris via email at pastor_chris@evangelismcoach.org for more information on these services.

Review Request

By now, you know how important Church Greeters Ministry can be to a local church. It is my hope that you have been inspired and energized with new ideas about how you can lead your greeter ministry to the next level. If you enjoyed this book or found it helpful to your ministry, I'd appreciate a review. Your support really does matter and makes a difference. I read all reviews that I receive and know about.

If you bought the PDF of this book, you can email me your review or suggestions to pastor_chris@evangelismcoach.org.

If you bought this from Amazon or another retailer (beginning in June 2013), visit the book site on Amazon where you'll see the big "Write a Review" – Click that and you are good to go. Here is the direct link to the Amazon page: http://www.amazon.com/dp/B00D5KN1BC.

Thanks again for your support,

Chris Walker, EvangelismCoach.org

Get a free download copy of my special report

7 Secrets to Great Church Hospitality at

WWW.EVANGELISMCOACH.ORG/7Secrets

and look for the signup box.

Made in the USA
Lexington, KY
17 March 2014